GREAT AMERICAN ENTREPRENEURS

# Andrew Carnegie

*Industrialist
and Philanthropist*

Kaitlin Scirri

Cavendish
Square
New York

*To Jenna, Brian, and Hannah, three of the greatest thinkers I know.*

Published in 2020 by Cavendish Square Publishing, LLC
243 5th Avenue, Suite 136, New York, NY 10016

First Edition

Website: cavendishsq.com

This publication represents the opinions and views of the author based on his or her personal experience, knowledge, and research. The information in this book serves as a general guide only. The author and publisher have used their best efforts in preparing this book and disclaim liability rising directly or indirectly from the use and application of this book.

All websites were available and accurate when this book was sent to press.

Names: Scirri, Kaitlin
Title: Andrew Carnegie: industrialist and philanthropist / Kaitlin Scirri.
Description: New York : Cavendish Square, 2019. |
Series: Great American entrepreneurs | Includes glossary and index.
Identifiers: ISBN 9781502648891 (pbk.) | ISBN 9781502648907 (library bound) |
ISBN 9781502648914 (ebook)
Subjects: LCSH: Carnegie, Andrew, 1835-1919--Juvenile literature. | Industrialists--United States--Biography--Juvenile literature. | Philanthropists--United States--Biography--Juvenile literature.
Classification: LCC CT275.C3 S33 2019 | DDC 361.7'4092 B--dc23

Editorial Director: David McNamara
Editor: Kristen Susienka
Copy Editor: Alex Tessman
Associate Art Director: Alan Sliwinski
Designer: Joseph Parenteau
Production Coordinator: Karol Szymczuk
Photo Research: J8 Media

Printed in the United States of America

# CONTENTS

# Strategic Businessman and Philanthropist

America was still a young nation when Andrew Carnegie arrived with his family in the mid-nineteenth century. Having declared their independence from the king of England, the Founding Fathers had established the United States of America with thirteen colonies. By the time the Carnegie family had arrived in 1848, America had grown physically as well as economically. The Industrial Revolution was under way and the Carnegies were among tens of thousands of immigrants hoping to build a new life in America, a land offering hope and prosperity.

## Working and Fighting in America

Andrew Carnegie found work quickly after arriving in America as a bobbin boy in a cotton factory. His hours

This portrait shows Andrew Carnegie in his later years, after achieving great financial success.

were long and the labor was tough, but he learned the value of hard work. He found himself being promoted rapidly through various factory and telegraph positions until he took a job working for the Pennsylvania Railroad. The job at the railroad would have a large impact on Carnegie's career and life.

When the country erupted into the Civil War, Carnegie went to Washington, DC, to serve in the War Department's telegraph office. He was honored to serve the country that had provided him so many opportunities for success.

## An Investor and Businessman

Following the war, Carnegie learned about the business of making financial investments and soon made some investments of his own. They proved profitable, and Carnegie's career continued to thrive. Using his knowledge of the railroad industry, Carnegie decided that iron and steel were the future of the country. He started his own iron company and eventually formed the Carnegie Steel Company. He joined other successful industrialists of the nineteenth century, including J. P. Morgan and John D. Rockefeller.

Although Carnegie encountered some obstacles throughout his career, such as criticisms of his business practices and a violent strike at one of his steel mills, he persevered and went on to dominate the steel industry.

## Carnegie's Writings and Legacy

Throughout his adult life, Carnegie took pleasure in writing and kept many journals. He wrote several books, including *Triumphant Democracy*, a tribute to the country that had proven to be very prosperous for him. He also penned an autobiography

Carnegie (*first row, center*) is seen here with social activist Booker T. Washington (*first row, left of Carnegie*) and others at the Tuskegee Institute, a prominent institution of higher learning for African Americans.

in his later years, but it was not published during his lifetime. Carnegie's most well-known written work was a book titled *The Gospel of Wealth*. In this piece, Carnegie expressed his belief that the wealthy were merely temporary guardians of their fortunes. He believed that the wealthy had an obligation to share their money with those who were less fortunate. Making good on his word, Carnegie sold his steel company to J. P. Morgan in 1901 and spent his retirement years giving away his fortune.

Carnegie's legacy is often summarized by his great success in the steel industry. He was so successful that he became one of the wealthiest men to ever live. But Carnegie's legacy is tied less to his great wealth and more to the fact that he gave it all away. His philanthropy is the legacy he is known for today. Several of the institutions, schools, libraries, and foundations that Carnegie started or funded during his lifetime are still in existence, continuing his charitable work and legacy.

# CHAPTER ONE

## A New and Growing Nation

America was formed in 1776 when the Founding Fathers declared independence from Great Britain. The American Revolution was fought from 1775 to 1783 to secure that independence. The Americans were victorious and were granted their freedom from the king of England's rule with the signing of the Treaty of Paris. Their new country offered promises of freedom and prosperity. However, America was a new nation and many challenges lay ahead. Americans had to fight to expand their country physically and work hard to grow the country's economy.

Many people, like the people shown here, immigrated to America in the 1800s with hope of freedom and prosperity.

## Growing Pains

Winning freedom from Great Britain was only the first step in developing a new country. Having reigned victorious in the American Revolution, Americans once again found themselves drawing battle lines with Great Britain in the War of 1812. Great Britain was already at war with France, which was under the rule of Napoleon. Great Britain involved America in the war when they attempted to restrict American trade and began to approach American ships. On June 1, 1812, US president James Madison requested a declaration of war from Congress. The war was fought from 1812 to 1815, and many American lives were lost. In addition to the loss of life, Americans endured a great deal of physical damage to their country. In August 1814, British soldiers marched into Washington, DC, and burned down the White House and other government buildings. The war ended with the signing of the Treaty of Ghent in Ghent, Belgium, on December 24, 1814. Rather than America or Great Britain gaining territory as a result of the war, they simply agreed to stop fighting and leave everything as it was prior to the start of the war. The war was over, and the loss was greater than the gain.

By the mid-nineteenth century, America was beginning to expand physically. The country, which had started with thirteen colonies, was growing and adding new territory. The United States doubled in size when it purchased the Louisiana Territory from France in 1803. The Louisiana Purchase also provided a means for the country to expand westward and has been referred to as the "greatest real estate deal in history."[1] The annexation of Texas by the United States in 1845 resulted in a dispute between the United States and Mexico. When the Americans annexed Texas, they claimed the territory as part of the United States and not Mexico. The two countries disagreed about exactly where the Texas border ended and how much territory the United States was able to claim. This dispute resulted in another war for the United States, and the Mexican-American War was fought from 1846 to 1848. America's victory over Mexico allowed the country to expand even further. America soon acquired the additional territories of California and New Mexico.

## The Industrial Revolution

By the 1770s, British manufacturers had learned the advantages of mechanization. Mechanization means that physical work traditionally done by hand was being done by machines instead. Water and steam power were being used to run new machines that could spin and weave cotton faster than workers could by hand. Factories were being built to house the machines, which could produce cotton of a better quality than hand-spun cotton. The machines also made the cotton cheaper to produce, allowing more of a profit once the cotton was sold.

The Americans had lost access to British manufacturers during the American Revolution and had to find their own ways to create these machines. British citizens were forbidden to share any secrets of industrialization with the Americans and were threatened with severe consequences if they did so. Soon, industrialists, or people who helped to create and profit from machine-powered industry, began to emerge. In 1789, an English industrialist named Samuel Slater was drawn to America in the hopes of being rewarded for bringing these new machines to the country. Fearful of being caught giving information to the Americans, he left all his plans and information about the new machines behind in England. Once in America, Slater

The arrival of industrialization in America brought the building of factories. Men, women, and children all became factory workers. They operated machines and performed manual labor, like the workers depicted here. These workers are processing pig iron at a factory in Alabama.

relied upon his memory to recreate the cotton-spinning and -weaving machines. As a result of his efforts, the first American factory opened in Rhode Island around 1790. The number of American factories increased over the next decade, and by 1815 there were over two hundred American factories.

The industrialization of the country affected American workers greatly. Industrialization is what happens when a large amount of mechanization occurs in one area. Prior to the invention of these machines, workers had the power and influence to fight for better wages and working conditions as they had been the ones performing all the work. But with machines able to stand in for workers, fewer skills were needed from individuals and their power and influence declined. As a result, there were strikes to protest wages and production expectations. A strike is when a group of workers agrees to stop production as a form of protest. Also initiated during this time were efforts to form workers' unions to protect workers' interests.

With the new machines being easily operable, women and children became common factory workers. Children were able to fit into small spaces that adults could not, which made them ideal for operating certain machines. Children working was a common practice during this time. Many people appreciated children being offered factory jobs, as it helped contribute to the household income while keeping the children out of trouble.

This industrialization of America had many positive effects on the country, including making Americans less reliant on foreign goods. American cities with factories attracted large numbers of citizens looking for work. As a result, the farm areas around the factory cities benefited from the opportunity to feed such large and growing populations.

Although most factories were built in the northern part of the country, the southern part of the country also played an important role in industrialization. The cotton factories in the North needed cotton to operate. While the southern United States had successfully grown cotton, separating the seeds from the cotton lint had proven to be a difficult and very time-consuming task. In 1793, Eli Whitney revolutionized the cotton industry when he invented the cotton gin. The cotton gin was an engine with wire teeth that rotated to separate the cotton lint from the cotton seeds. With the use of a cotton gin, productivity in cotton cleaning increased greatly. The cotton from the South was used to stimulate the country's economy through use in the factories and through exporting to other countries.

## Innovations and Inventions

The early 1800s saw several innovations, or new ideas and new methods of working, and corresponding inventions that had a profound impact on the United States. In 1835, Samuel F. B. Morse invented Morse Code. Morse Code is a coding system in which dots and dashes were used in place of numbers and letters. In 1837, Morse received a patent on an electromagnetic telegraph. A telegraph was a way to send a message across a long distance using signals from an electric device. Through a telegraph, one could send a message using Morse Code through a machine and the message would be copied onto a piece of paper. The United States government offered financial support to Morse, and in 1843, it allowed him to build a telegraph system between Washington, DC, and Baltimore, Maryland. The system was successful, and on May 24, 1844, the first telegraph was transmitted with the message, "What

# THE ERIE CANAL

As the United States grew and expanded, a way to move goods and passengers throughout the country was necessary. Many goods arrived via the Atlantic Ocean and would then travel from New York City up the Hudson River. But moving the goods west, through the Appalachian Mountains, posed a problem. DeWitt Clinton, governor of New York in the early 1800s, proposed building a canal that would link the Hudson River with Lake Erie by the city of Buffalo, New York. After encountering some opposition to his idea, Clinton raised funds to finance the project, and construction on the canal began in 1817.

The canal was dug by hand and completed in 1825. It helped to accelerate westward expansion of the United States as people and goods were now able to reach major cities like Chicago, Detroit, and Cleveland. The Erie Canal provided the backdrop to many historical American events, such as the first women's rights convention held in Seneca Falls, New York. It was also used as part of the Underground Railroad to bring slaves to freedom in the North and in Canada.

Canal traffic remained the main transportation used for passengers and goods until the arrival of the railroad. While the canal remained the less expensive mode of transportation, it could not compete with the railroad's speed. Today, the Erie Canal still exists, a landmark of American expansionism.

hath God wrought!"[2] The telegraph became the dominant form of communication in the United States.

Until the early 1800s, most goods and produce were moved throughout the country on the Mississippi River. Barges and other vessels carried items long distances. This changed in 1825 with the completion of the Erie Canal. This new outlet allowed goods and produce from the west to move quicker to the east.

However, the East Coast of the country was still not able to connect with the country's interior. The solution was the Pennsylvania Railroad. In 1846, the Pennsylvania legislature approved the Pennsylvania Railroad. By 1856, the railroad reached as far as Chicago. It would grow to be a success for the state of Pennsylvania as well as the entire United States.

## Immigration

In addition to growing physically and economically, the country was growing in terms of population. More Americans were being born on American soil, and a great number of immigrants were coming to America with hopes of freedom and prosperity. Immigration in America increased after 1815 with the end of the War of 1812 and the defeat of French leader Napoleon Bonaparte. An estimated 150,000 European immigrants arrived in America in the 1820s, an estimated 600,000 in the 1830s, and over 1 million in the 1840s.

There were various reasons that people were drawn to America. Many were attracted to the freedoms the country offered, including political and religious freedoms, while some favored the idea of economic opportunity and prosperity. In some cases, others had little choice but to leave their homelands due to economic uncertainty and lack of adequate living supplies. This was especially true for Irish immigrants who faced the Great Famine of 1845 to 1849. In Ireland, the potato was the dominant crop, and the Irish depended on it for their survival. During the Great Famine, the potato crops failed to produce for several years in a row. The lack of potato crops brought starvation to the Irish and forced many of them to flee their homeland. As a result, many came to call America their new home.

Immigration in America also coincided with the growth of manufacturing in America. Many Europeans were attracted to the jobs being created through America's industrial growth. Many European immigrants were young, strong, and willing to work factory jobs. This created resentment among many American factory workers. As a result, many prejudices developed between Americans and immigrants, and even between different immigrant groups.

## The Age of Reform

As a new and growing country, America experienced periods of unrest and disagreement among its citizens. The period of 1830 to 1850 is referred to as the Age of Reform because a variety of movements were taking place during that time in an effort to bring about various reforms, or changes, to the country. These movements were largely in the northern part of the country. Some of the movements that emerged during this time included women's rights, slaves' rights, pacifism, temperance, and better conditions for the working class. Pacifism is a belief that violence is an unnecessary and unacceptable means of solving disagreements. Pacifists encouraged peaceful resolutions to disputes. Temperance was a call to moderation in behavior and specifically called for alcohol abstinence.

## Women's Rights and Slaves' Rights

One reform movement in the North was that of slaves' rights. Many people wanted to see slavery abolished, or made illegal, but if that were not possible, then they wanted to see an improvement in the treatment of slaves. Reformers disagreed with slave families being torn apart and the lack of education given to slaves. They urged slave owners who refused to give up their slaves to treat their slaves humanely.

Many reformers were women who fought for slaves' rights and also supported women's rights. In speaking out against slavery, women encountered resistance from those who believed that women should not speak in public. Some of these people were fellow reformers fighting to end slavery. Although they wanted slavery to end, they did not want women getting involved. Women were expected to fulfill their roles as wives and mothers and not involve themselves with political affairs. Women fighting for equality often cited the Declaration of Independence, which stated all men were created equal. They argued that it should state that all men *and women* were created equal so that the freedoms that come with being an American citizen would encompass all citizens, not just men.

In July 1848, Elizabeth Cady Stanton and Lucretia Mott, two key players in the fight for women's equality, organized a meeting called the Seneca Falls Convention, in Seneca Falls, New York. Stanton and Mott drafted their own document, called the Declaration of Sentiments, in which they stated, "We hold these truths to be self-evident: that all men and women are created equal."[3] Using Thomas Jefferson's Declaration of Independence as a model, the Declaration of Sentiments listed the ways in which women were being

Susan B. Anthony, an important figure in the women's rights and slaves' rights movements, is seen here sitting at her desk around the late 1860s.

oppressed by a patriarchal society, just as Jefferson had listed the ways in which King George III had been oppressing the American colonists in 1776. Patriarchy is a society in which men are dominant. The women's suffrage movement, or right to vote movement, grew. It attracted both women and men, and several national conventions were held.

A strong voice to emerge from the women's suffrage movement was that of Susan B. Anthony. She became one of the most influential and hard-working supporters of women's rights. Anthony spoke out for women's rights as well as abolition, becoming a member of the American Anti-Slavery Society in 1856. Anthony endured open hostility toward her, as well as threats of violence as she spoke out on behalf of equality for women and freedom for slaves. In 1868, Anthony began publishing her own newspaper in Rochester, New York, called the *Revolution*. In her paper, she called for equal rights of all American citizens.

One of the most famous and influential abolitionists, Frederick Douglass is seen here in 1848. Douglass, a former slave himself, dedicated his life to gaining freedom for all slaves.

## Abolitionism

By the mid-1800s, slavery had become a heavily debated issue in the United States. Abolitionism was a movement in which many people worked to end slavery. These people were known as abolitionists. The Fifth Amendment was often cited by abolitionists, as it stated that no one could be deprived of "life, liberty, or property, without due process of law."[4] Advocates for the ending of slavery used this quote to argue that slavery was unconstitutional. However, proponents of slavery counterargued that slaves were property and not American citizens with rights of their own.

One American who fervently believed in the emancipation of slaves was William Lloyd Garrison. Garrison organized the New England Anti-Slavery Society in 1831 and created a newspaper called the *Liberator*. Garrison called for an immediate end to slavery. He was also a supporter of women's rights, and his views on these two subjects caused outrage among many citizens. He received threats of violence, and in 1835, he was attacked by an angry mob.

It was not only white citizens who were working toward freedom for slaves but black citizens as well. Some of them had been former slaves themselves. One such man was Frederick Douglass. Douglass had escaped from slavery and settled in Massachusetts. There he became involved in the antislavery movement and joined the Massachusetts Anti-Slavery Society. He often did public-speaking engagements at the society's meetings, where he would recount for the audience what it was like to be a slave. Although he suffered violence as a slave, he did learn to read and write. This was a rarity, as most slaves were kept uneducated. Douglass used his literacy skills to tell his story, and in 1845, he published his autobiography, titled

*Narrative of the Life of Frederick Douglass.* Douglass broke the stereotype of the uneducated, unintelligent slave who was incapable of learning. He proved that slaves could learn and display intellect, thought, and reasoning just as any white man could. In fact, some of his white supporters expressed concern that Douglass appeared and sounded too educated. They thought that people might think him an imposter and not really a former slave. They suggested that Douglass alter his speech so as to sound more like a slave was expected to sound, with more limited vocabulary and a heavier accent. Douglass did not listen to these suggestions and continued his fight to end slavery in America.

With all of its political unrest, the Age of Reform helped to usher in a period of great division in the country. This is particularly true of the abolitionist movement and the antislavery sentiments being expressed throughout the North. Brewing tensions laid the groundwork for another war, only this time not with a foreign power. The United States Civil War was on the horizon, in which the country would divide between North and South and fight against itself in an effort to end the slavery debate once and for all.

## An Ocean Away

Across the Atlantic Ocean from America lay the country of Scotland. Scotland was a country with much upheaval of its own in the mid-nineteenth century. During that time, large waves of immigration took place in which Scottish citizens left their home country for other countries. Motivation for immigrating varied, but for many people it was the hope of improving their quality of life that caused them to leave. In large areas of Scotland, the land was hard and rocky and not ideal for growing crops. With no crops to sell, farmers could earn no money. An alternative to growing crops was fishing, but when that failed to yield results, citizens faced the risk of starvation. With the introduction of steam-powered machines in the late 1700s, the linen industry faced high rates of unemployment as hand workers were replaced by machines. Hand workers were thrust into poverty and faced poor living conditions for themselves and their families. Many Scottish citizens chose to leave these grim conditions behind and immigrate to America, with hopes of a better life. One such family was that of Andrew Carnegie, a man who would become infamous in the United States and around the world.

Carnegie's Birthplace, Dunfermline

75619 JY

# CHAPTER TWO

# From Rags to Riches

T hough Andrew Carnegie's name has become synonymous with wealth and prosperity, his beginnings in Scotland offer a sharp contrast to the image of a successful businessman and wealthy philanthropist that he is remembered as today.

## Humble Beginnings

Named after his grandfather, Andrew Carnegie was born in Dunfermline, Scotland, on November 25, 1835, to William Carnegie and Margaret Morrison Carnegie. William was a handweaver of cotton, and the family lived in Dunfermline because of its linen industry. While

Carnegie was born in humble circumstances in Dunfermline, Scotland, before immigrating to America in 1848.

the family was not wealthy, William was a successful weaver and the family owned multiple looms in their home. When Carnegie was eight years old, his younger brother, Tom, arrived to complete the Carnegie family.

Carnegie began attending school in Scotland around age eight after requesting of his parents that he be allowed to do so. He loved learning and reveled in his school lessons, as well as those of Scotland's history that he received from his uncle Lauder. As a result of these history lessons, Carnegie developed a great sense of Scottish pride. By age twelve, he could read, write, and do basic math.

Dunfermline was teeming with political activity during Carnegie's childhood. At times he would go to hear his father speak at political meetings and rallies. A firm belief of the Carnegie family was that privilege was not necessary. They believed in equality, that no one should struggle financially while others around them were indulging. This belief was gaining a strong following in some political circles in Scotland. This message was one that Carnegie heard his father speak passionately about in public meetings as he worked to change their society. He believed in better conditions for workers and spoke out as a political reformer. His message of equality, of doing away with wealthy privilege, would stay with Carnegie throughout his life.

Steam-powered machines were becoming common, and when handlooms were replaced by steam looms, William found himself out of work. Margaret took it upon herself to find work to help support the family. But even with Margaret contributing to the household income, things got more and more difficult financially. Finally, the family was forced to entertain the idea of sailing for America, for a chance to start over in a new country full of opportunities.

Carnegie's aunt and uncle had previously sailed for America, leaving Carnegie and his family behind in Scotland. As a boy, Carnegie would look at a map of America and picture the "land of promise" that they had sailed for.[1] Many immigrants found hope in America during the mid-nineteenth century, and the Carnegies were no different. Carnegie's uncle and father in particular regarded "the superiority of America ... a home for freemen in which every citizen's privilege was every man's right."[2] For the Carnegies, America meant a place of equality, where everyone would have the opportunity to earn a good wage, support their families, and prosper, not just the wealthy. When Carnegie was twelve years old, he set sail on a seven-week journey to America with his mother, father, and little brother.

## Coming to America

When the Carnegies arrived in America in 1848, the country consisted of thirty states. Wisconsin had become the thirtieth state on May 29, 1848. Zachary Taylor was elected the twelfth president later that year. The Industrial Revolution had created a multitude of manufacturing jobs, and immigrants like the Carnegies were arriving by the tens of thousands. The women's rights and abolitionist movements were under way. It was an exciting yet turbulent time to be in America.

The Carnegies learned upon their arrival that canals were the main source of transportation over long distances. Carnegie and his family took the Erie Canal to travel west of New York City. They settled in Allegheny City, Pennsylvania. They already had family living there and were able to live in family-owned rooms free of charge. William took up handweaving again and often traveled to sell his work. Margaret once again pitched in to help support the family and worked as a shoe binder for local shoemakers, sewing parts of shoes together using needle and thread. She earned the family $4 ($119 in 2018) a week for her work.

With a multitude of manufacturing jobs available in America, William ultimately gave up his handweaving and decided to find factory work instead. He began work at a cotton factory, and as children were often employed by factory owners, he also secured a job for Carnegie as a bobbin boy. Carnegie's job was to bring bobbins, or small cylinders of thread or yarn, to the workers running the looms. He earned $1.20 ($34 in 2018) a week for his work. Carnegie later recalled his experiences as a bobbin boy in his autobiography:

> The hours hung heavily upon me and in the work itself I took no pleasure; but the cloud had a silver lining, as it gave me the feeling that I was doing something for my world—our family. I have made millions since, but none of those millions gave me such a happiness as my first week's earnings.[3]

While working as a bobbin boy meant long days and hard work, Carnegie loved the feeling of contributing to his family's income. He learned early on the satisfaction that came from being rewarded for his hard work.

## A Hard Worker

After working as a bobbin boy, Carnegie was able to secure a job working for a bobbin manufacturer. This position came with a substantial pay increase, and Carnegie began bringing home $2 ($59 in 2018) a week. When Carnegie's employer realized

Carnegie's first job was as a bobbin boy in a textile factory. Bobbin boys, like the one pictured in this photograph, spent long days working hard. They would run around the factory, replacing thread and yarn for looms.

that he had an aptitude for numbers and finances, he allowed Carnegie to start handling his books, or accounts. Realizing that he had much he could learn in regards to bookkeeping and accounting, Carnegie, along with some friends, decided to attend night school together in Pittsburgh. In night school, they learned more complex forms of bookkeeping and accounting, which served them well in their jobs.

In 1850, two years after arriving in America, Carnegie was able to obtain a job as a telegraph messenger boy through a connection of his uncle's. His new job paid $2.50 ($75 in 2018) a week. His mother was pleased for him but his father was uncertain. He felt that Carnegie was too small and too

The Pennsylvania Railroad played an integral part in Carnegie's career, leading to employment, connections, and investments that helped him make his fortune. Here, a train is seen traveling on the Pennsylvania Railroad in the late 1890s.

young for such a job. But Carnegie accepted the position and found that he enjoyed it. It was at this job that Carnegie made some lasting friendships and also had the benefit of becoming acquainted with some of Pittsburgh's leading businessmen, connections that would prove beneficial later in his career.

Carnegie soon found himself with another new job when he was promoted to telegraph operator in 1851. He had learned

about telegraphs and how to operate them from his time in the telegraph office as a messenger boy. When a substitute telegraph operator was needed in a nearby city, he jumped at the chance to try his hand in the field. He was successful and was promoted to telegraph operator upon his return to Pittsburgh. At age sixteen, Carnegie was making $25 ($748 in 2018) a month, a sum that was considered a fortune to him and his family.

Two years later, in 1853, Carnegie accepted a position as a clerk and telegraph operator for Thomas A. Scott. Scott was the superintendent of the telegraph department of the Pennsylvania Railroad. As superintendent, Scott oversaw all of the operations of the railroad. He would come to be a mentor to Carnegie and a personal friend throughout much of Carnegie's life. As payment for working for Scott, Carnegie earned the most he had ever made—$35 ($1,047 in 2018) a month. In this position, Carnegie witnessed the rapid growth of the telegraph business. In 1859, when Scott was promoted, Carnegie was appointed superintendent. New telegraph offices were being built, and more telegraph operators were needed. Carnegie and his co-superintendent were among the first to hire women as telegraph operators, believing them to be more reliable than young men.

Amid Carnegie's hard work and success, the Carnegie family was dealt a difficult loss when William Carnegie succumbed to illness and died on October 2, 1855. Once again, Margaret Carnegie stepped in to help support her family by binding shoes. Tom focused on his education, attending the local public school, and Carnegie kept his job working for Mr. Scott at the Pennsylvania Railroad. With the death of his father, Carnegie had become the head of the Carnegie household, and he felt a responsibility to provide for his mother and younger brother.

# IMMIGRATION IN AMERICA

During the nineteenth and early twentieth centuries, the United States experienced a wave of immigration. However, newcomers were often disliked because of their cultural customs and were accused of stealing jobs from Americans. This fear of people from different countries was called xenophobia. However, it did not stop people from moving there.

After the Civil War, some states began passing anti-immigration laws. Immigration became a federal responsibility following an 1875 Supreme Court ruling. The first law to restrict immigration came in 1882 after an increase in Chinese immigration resulted in anti-Chinese sentiments, particularly in California, where most of the Chinese immigrants had settled. Tensions rose and the West Coast was in a state of upheaval. As a result, Congress passed the Chinese Exclusion Act. This prohibited Chinese laborers from immigrating to the United States for a period of ten years. It was later extended before being made permanent in 1902.

Ellis Island was the most well-known immigration station. It opened on January 1, 1892, and processed over twelve million immigrants before officially closing in 1954. In 1965, it became a national monument. It is now open to the public as an immigration museum. Also in 1965, Congress passed the Immigration and Naturalization Act, which did away with limiting immigration by a certain number of immigrants, specific to the country of origin. Immigration limits for certain nationalities had been commonly instated and capped in decades past. Instead, the focus of immigration shifted to refugees fleeing violence in other countries, immigrants with skills that could prove useful to the United States, and the family members of people who had already immigrated to America.

Today, many people still desire to come to the United States—to get an education, find work, or escape political unrest in their homeland. The US government has developed processes to allow immigrants to move there. One process involves applying for a green card. This means immigrants must register with the United States government. Once approved, a green card lets immigrants live and work in the United States. Every year, the US government receives approximately six million applications for entry into the United States.

# A Country at War

The Carnegies had been in America for over a decade when tension between the Northern states and the Southern states was coming to a head. The Northern free states wanted to abolish slavery, while the Southern slave states wanted to keep their slaves. This national disagreement culminated in 1860 with the election of Abraham Lincoln as the sixteenth president. Lincoln campaigned on a promise to keep slavery out of the territories that had not become states yet. His election was concerning to many Southerners. Shortly after Lincoln won the presidency, seven slave states seceded from the United States of America and formed the Confederate States of America. When the states seceded, they officially withdrew themselves from the United States and declared themselves no longer part of the country. The seven states to initially secede were Alabama, Florida, Georgia, Louisiana, Mississippi, South Carolina, and Texas. After violence erupted at Fort Sumter on April 12, 1861, Arkansas, North Carolina, Tennessee, and Virginia also seceded and joined the Confederacy.

Andrew Carnegie was twenty-six years old and still employed by the Pennsylvania Railroad when the Civil War began. He did not fight in battle but instead put his telegraph skills to use in Washington, DC, on behalf of the Union army. In 1861, Thomas Scott was named assistant secretary of war in charge of the Transportation Department, and he called for Carnegie to join him. Carnegie served as Scott's assistant and was in charge of the military railroads and government telegraphs. His duties included traveling to repair downed telegraph wires to restore communication, which was of the utmost importance during the war. He also joined workers night and day as they rushed to extend railroad tracks that were needed to transport Union

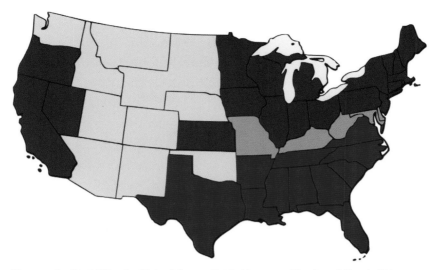

During the Civil War, the United States divided between North and South. This map shows the division, with Southern Confederate states in red and Northern Union states in blue. The light blue states allowed slavery but sided with the Union. They are sometimes called "border states."

soldiers to battle and transport wounded soldiers to be treated. Carnegie was grateful to be of service to the country that had provided such opportunity and fortune to him.

Carnegie's service to the War Department did not last long. When he was initially summoned to Washington, DC, it was thought that the war would be short-lived. However, it was soon predicted to last years. Mr. Scott and Carnegie needed to return to their positions at the railroad in Pittsburgh. The government was placing heavy demands upon the railroad for the war effort, and the Pennsylvania Railroad could not spare them for such a length of time. Permanent workers replaced them in Washington, DC, and Carnegie and Scott returned to Pittsburgh.

In 1864, Carnegie was drafted, or called to service, by the Union army. He had the choice of finding someone to report in his place or paying a fee of $300 ($4,694 in 2018), a large amount of money at the time. The $300 fee would get Carnegie out of one call to service, but he could later be called to service again, depending on the duration of the war. Carnegie believed he had already done his duty to America in serving at his Washington, DC, post with the telegraph office. He decided to pay someone $850 ($13,299 in 2018) to report for duty in his place so he would not be called to service any more during the war. Paying someone to serve in your place was a common practice at the time for those who could afford to do so.

The Civil War did indeed last years, until 1865. The war ended after the Confederate army surrendered to the Union army. Confederate commander Robert E. Lee surrendered to Ulysses S. Grant, Union army general and future president of the United States, in April 1865. Realizing the collapse of the Confederacy was imminent, Confederate president Jefferson Davis attempted to flee Union soldiers. But he was captured on May 10, 1865, and the Civil War concluded. On December 6, 1865, the Thirteenth Amendment to the United States Constitution, which abolished slavery, was ratified, or formally adopted.

## A Businessman

Andrew Carnegie had learned in his years since coming to America the value of hard work. He had applied himself in each of his positions and, as a result, was promoted and rewarded with higher-paying positions and greater responsibilities. While working for Mr. Scott at the Pennsylvania Railroad, he made his first financial investment. A financial investment is when one puts money into a business or idea, hoping to receive a profit in return. It was Scott who taught Carnegie about investing, a foreign idea to the young man. Carnegie had worked for every cent he had ever earned. The idea of earning money without doing any physical labor was strange to him. Yet, he made an investment based on Scott's advice and was shocked and pleased when his investment yielded a profit. In his autobiography, Carnegie recalled his reaction to learning of the money he had made on his first financial investment, saying, "It gave me the first penny of revenue from capital—something that I had not worked for with the sweat of my brow. 'Eureka!' I cried. 'Here's the goose that lays the golden eggs.'"[4] Capital is money that someone has that can be turned into more money through financial or business investments. In Carnegie's case, he had taken out a mortgage on his newly purchased house in order to have enough capital to invest in the stocks Scott had suggested. It was a gamble that paid off.

Carnegie would soon make another investment, this time in a new type of railroad car. Railroad travel had become common, but there were no accommodations for overnight travel. Carnegie was approached by Theodore Woodruff, who had designed a new kind of railroad car. It was called a sleeper car and included beds to make passengers more comfortable during overnight travel. Carnegie saw an opportunity and invested in the sleeper cars, which proved to be another profitable investment for him.

With the money he made from his investment in sleeper cars, Carnegie decided to make another investment, this time in oil. In the mid-1800s, oil had been discovered in Pennsylvania. On August 27, 1859, the first successful oil well was drilled by American Edwin Drake in Titusville, Pennsylvania. In 1862, Carnegie invested in an oil well in that state. His investment was so profitable that he later invested in another oil well in Ohio.

Carnegie Steel became the largest supplier of steel in the world. One of Carnegie's largest steel plants is seen here in Homestead, Pennsylvania.

Following the Civil War, Carnegie realized that wooden bridges were to become a thing of the past. They caught fire too easily and burned to the ground, causing damage and delays in travel. He concluded that iron and steel bridges were the future and founded the Keystone Bridge Company in 1865. The company was very successful, building numerous bridges in America, the most notable being the Eads Bridge in St. Louis, Missouri, in 1874. The following year, Carnegie opened his first steel plant in Braddock, Pennsylvania, named Edgar Thomson Steel Works. In 1883, Carnegie purchased Homestead Steel Works, and over the following years, he began to overtake his competition in the steel industry. In 1892, he formed the Carnegie Steel Company, which became the largest supplier of steel in the world. In 1901, Carnegie sold his steel company to financier J. P. Morgan for $480 million (over $14 billion in 2018) and retired as one of the wealthiest men in the world.

## Written Works

Carnegie wrote a lot during his lifetime and published several books. He developed his reading and writing skills as a child in Scotland and as a young man in America. He had a great appreciation for books and believed writing was an excellent way to express his feelings on business, wealth, and later, his own life. His published works include *An American Four-in-Hand in Britain* in 1883, about a trip he took with friends through the British countryside; *Triumphant Democracy* in 1886, in which he called on Britain to learn from America's democracy; a collection of essays titled *The Empire of Business* in 1902; and his autobiography, which was published in 1920 after his death. One of his most famous and most quoted

Andrew Carnegie and his wife, Louise Whitfield, are photographed here around the late 1800s.

works was an essay he wrote in 1889 titled "Wealth," in which he called on the wealthy to share their money with the less fortunate. This essay was later published in 1900 as the book *The Gospel of Wealth*.

## Family Life

The Carnegies were a tightly knit family. Having very little financial resources, they had learned to work hard, pitch in, and rely on each other to survive. William Carnegie's death in 1855 pulled the surviving Carnegies even closer together, with Margaret and Carnegie taking over financial responsibilities for the family. It was a great joy to Carnegie when he had made enough money to hire a servant to help his mother with household tasks. Providing his mother and his brother Tom with a better life was a great motivator for Carnegie in his endeavors, and he enjoyed sharing his success with his family.

In 1886, Carnegie contracted typhoid fever. Typhoid fever was a bacterial infection of the stomach that was common during the Civil War era. Not long after, his brother Tom caught pneumonia. While Carnegie ultimately recovered from his sickness, his brother succumbed to his. Three weeks later, Carnegie's mother Margaret also passed away.

The loss of his mother and brother was extremely painful for Carnegie, and he sought comfort in a friend, Louise Whitfield. Carnegie and Whitfield had been friends for quite some time, having met when he was forty-five and she twenty-three. Eventually, their friendship budded into romance, much to his mother's dismay.

Carnegie and Whitfield would often go horseback riding together in New York City's Central Park. By this time in his life, Carnegie had proven himself to be a very successful businessman. He was well known and quite wealthy. However, this status was not appealing to Whitfield. She felt that Carnegie's great wealth left no room for her, that she would not be needed in any way. Whitfield's father had been reliant on her mother in many ways, and Whitfield wanted the same thing in her own marriage. She maintained these feelings for a long time, and at one point returned letters Carnegie had written her and advised him that she could not marry him. To make matters worse, Margaret did not approve of the match and often tried to break the couple apart.

After Margaret and Tom died, Whitfield saw Carnegie's devastation and realized that he needed her. Carnegie, in turn, realized he was all alone in the world now, and above all, he wanted no one else but "Lou." Whitfield and Carnegie were married in her family home on April 22, 1887. Carnegie was fifty-one years old and Whitfield thirty years old.

Carnegie and Whitfield had one child together, a daughter named Margaret. She was born on March 30, 1897, almost ten years after they had married. They named her as a tribute to Carnegie's mother.

## Retirement and Legacy

After selling Carnegie Steel to J. P. Morgan in 1901, he entered retirement. Sixty-five years old and no longer a working man, he was finally able to devote his time and money to philanthropy, or generous financial donations to others. His childhood lessons from his father about wealthy privilege had stayed with him throughout his life. He made an effort to make charitable donations whenever his income allowed him to do so, and he firmly believed that the wealthy had an obligation to help those less fortunate. In *The Gospel of Wealth*, Carnegie shared his belief that "the man who dies thus rich dies disgraced."[5] For many years, he had planned on spending his retirement years giving away his fortune. He was so determined to do so that he requested that his wife sign an agreement before they were married stating that she understood and agreed with Carnegie's decision to give away most of his money. He did not want to die a wealthy man. He wanted to see his money going to good use and helping the less fortunate. Whitfield agreed with him and supported him in this endeavor.

His earliest philanthropic contributions were given during his career when he gave money toward the opening of several public libraries. Carnegie had a lifelong love of books and reading. When he was a child and his family struggled financially, he benefited greatly from libraries, as there was no extra money for him to buy books of his own. He longed to offer this opportunity to others and financed several libraries in America, as well as in his home country of Scotland. He also gave money to open several schools, museums, nonprofit organizations, and institutions dedicated to the arts, science, and supporting peace.

After his retirement, he and his wife spent time at their home in New York City, as well as time in Scotland. Carnegie spent much of his time outdoors golfing, fishing, and swimming. The Carnegies enjoyed traveling and entertaining, and counted many important and well-known figures as friends. They were acquainted with author Mark Twain, poet Matthew Arnold, and Theodore Roosevelt, the twenty-sixth president of the United States.

Toward the end of his life, Andrew Carnegie cited two regrets. First, that he was unable to give away his entire fortune. He had made hundreds of millions of dollars in charitable donations, but there was still money left over, money that he would have liked to see put to good use rather than sitting unused. His second regret was the lack of peace in the world. As a pacifist, Carnegie believed in nonviolent resolutions to problems. In 1910, he founded the Carnegie Endowment for International Peace with a $10 million (over $262 million in 2018) donation. His intention for the organization was to work toward abolishing international conflicts and wars. But when World War I broke out four years later, in 1914, Carnegie was left heartbroken. The war ended in 1918, and Carnegie died shortly after. He had endured a case of influenza and two serious cases of pneumonia, which had weakened him. He died on August 11, 1919, at the age of eighty-three. His story and legacy live on today through the multitude of schools, institutions, libraries, and organizations that he founded. They continue to work toward education, research, promoting the arts, and achieving peace.

# CHAPTER THREE

# Friends and Foes

The mid-nineteenth century saw the emergence of many great businessmen and industrialists. Andrew Carnegie acquired several friends and business acquaintances throughout his career, as well as some strained relationships.

## Henry Clay Frick

Henry Clay Frick was born in Pennsylvania in 1849, just one year after Andrew Carnegie and his family arrived in America. Like Carnegie, Frick enjoyed much success in his career as an industrialist. The two businessmen eventually developed a professional relationship, as both were invested in the iron and steel industry.

Carnegie is seen here at a labor conference in 1905 with other figures of his time. From left to right: Carnegie, William Jennings Bryan, James J. Hill, and John Mitchell.

## Frick and Carnegie

In 1871, Frick created his own company in which he supplied coke, an important raw material needed to make iron. He named his business Frick and Company and capitalized on the high demand for coke in the Pittsburgh iron and steel industry. His company was very successful, making Frick a millionaire by the time he was in his twenties. Frick was brought aboard Carnegie Brothers and Company in 1889 as their chairman, or the head of the business. Carnegie was hoping Frick could reorganize the business so that they could beat out their competitors. He was successful in his role and did manage to buy out Carnegie's largest competitor. This made Carnegie the world's largest steel supplier.

## The Homestead Strike

Carnegie and Frick had a good working relationship until the Homestead Strike on July 6, 1892. Prior to that time, Carnegie's steel business had experienced such success and demand that it required multiple steel mills. One of the largest mills was in Homestead, Pennsylvania. Carnegie placed Frick in charge of operations of the Homestead steel mill. The Homestead steel mill had a contract with a labor union, the Amalgamated Association of Iron and Steel Workers. The union ensured that certain conditions were met for the workers, like maintaining wage amounts and safe working conditions.

In the summer of 1892, the labor contract that the mill had with the union was close to expiring. Carnegie was out of the country visiting Scotland and had left Frick in charge of the mill, the laborers, and the contract negotiations.

Frick decided to cut the workers' wages, which caused an angry response from the laborers and the union. Rather than

This drawing illustrates the violence of the Homestead Strike that occurred at Carnegie's steel mill in Homestead, Pennsylvania, in 1892.

negotiate, Frick locked the workers out of the mill. He decided that they would work for the wages he was offering or they would not work at all. He then proceeded to fire all of the workers—over three thousand people—and brought in a team of security guards to protect the mill. However, the workers were angry and refused to go away quietly. On July 6, 1892, the fired workers, along with some of their families, stormed the mill and attacked the security guards. The security guards eventually surrendered to the angry crowd, and the workers took over the mill.

Desperate for control over the situation, Frick contacted the governor of Pennsylvania and asked for help. The governor responded by sending in the National Guard, a large US military force used to protect and assist the country. The strike resolved on July 12 when the fired laborers released the mill to the soldiers. The mill was opened again on July 15 with replacement workers taking over the jobs of the union strikers. The strike resulted in multiple deaths and countless injuries. At least three security guards and seven workers were killed.

Frick's life was also threatened as part of the strike conflict when a man named Alexander Berkman broke into his office and tried to shoot him. Berkman was not one of the strikers, but he did sympathize with their cause. Frick was wounded during the incident but survived.

After the Homestead Strike, Carnegie and Frick's relationship was strained, each having strong feelings about the violent battle and about each other's actions leading up to and during the strike. Carnegie felt that had he been at the Homestead steel mill himself, he could have prevented the strike from occurring.

# J. P. Morgan

Similarly to Andrew Carnegie, John Pierpont (J. P.) Morgan found financial success in America in the mid and late nineteenth century.

## Early Life and Career

Born in America in 1837, Morgan was educated in Massachusetts and started his financial career as an accountant at age twenty. Morgan's father, Junius Spencer Morgan, was already an established and respected banker in London and a business associate of Carnegie's. In 1869, Carnegie journeyed to London after establishing his Keystone Bridge Company. There, with the help of Junius Morgan, he made a lot of money selling mortgage bonds.

Back in America, J. P. Morgan worked his way up through his father's banking firms, and in 1871, he became a partner in the prominent firm of Drexel, Morgan, and Company in New York City. In 1895, the firm was renamed J. P. Morgan and Company and enjoyed immense success, often as a source of financing for the US government. During the time when railroads were the dominant means of transportation, Morgan orchestrated a compromise between the two largest competing railroads, the New York Central Railroad and the Pennsylvania Railroad. His success in coordinating their meeting averted a potentially disastrous battle between the two major railroads that could have resulted in dramatic rate increases. As a result of his success in railroad reorganization, Morgan gained a large portion of railroad stock, making him one of the wealthiest and most influential businessmen in the railroad industry.

Following his success with railroads, Morgan turned his financial talents toward industrialization. His financial firm

J. P. Morgan, seen here around 1890, purchased Carnegie Steel from Andrew Carnegie in 1901 to form the world's first billion-dollar corporation.

had previously financed Thomas Edison's efforts to make an electric lightbulb. In 1891, Morgan created General Electric by merging Edison General Electric and Thomson-Houston Electric Company. Having financed the Federal Steel Company in 1898, Morgan next sought to dominate the steel industry. He achieved his goal in 1901 when he purchased Carnegie Steel from Andrew Carnegie and merged it with his own steel company. He named his new company United States Steel Corporation, and it became the world's first billion-dollar corporation.

In the early twentieth century, Morgan shifted his efforts away from industrialization and focused instead on banks and insurance companies. His life's work had earned him a prominent position on the board of many influential and powerful companies. This gave his financial firm a lot of control and a position of power when it came to the country's leading financial institutions.

## Family and Legacy

After losing his first wife to tuberculosis in 1862, Morgan married a woman named Frances Louisa Tracy in 1865. The couple had four children together, including a son whom they named after Morgan. Morgan continued his career in the financial industry until he died in 1913.

Having developed a great appreciation for art during his lifetime, Morgan left his collection of books to the Morgan Library of New York. He left his fortune and business to his son, John Pierpont Morgan Jr., in the hopes of carrying forward the family financial legacy. In 2000, J. P. Morgan & Co. merged with the Chase Manhattan Company to form J. P. Morgan Chase & Co., which still exists today. The United States Steel Company also continues to exist, carrying forward the industrial legacies of Carnegie and Morgan.

# SOCIAL DARWINISM

Charles Darwin was an Englishman born in 1809. He studied natural history and developed his own theory of evolution, or his own idea of the way humans have changed throughout their existence. Darwin's *On the Origin of Species* was published in 1859. In his book, Darwin presented his theory that species survive over time by natural selection. This means that the species most adapted to survive in a certain environment, the one with the most survival skills, will continue to exist, reproduce, and thrive while other weaker species die out. The species that survives will continue to grow and change over time, adapting to its environment and developing the physical traits and skills that are needed to continue to exist.

Darwin's theory grew in popularity and began to be applied to circumstances other than survival for existence. His theory was adopted by businessmen and economists, who claimed that survival of the fittest could be applied to capitalism. The idea that the strongest and most skilled businessmen would beat out their competition to become the most successful was reasonable and acceptable to many Americans. This became known as social Darwinism.

Not everyone embraced social Darwinism, however, with reformers such as Henry George, Edward Bellamy, and Henry Demarest Lloyd denouncing it. They did not believe that survival of the fittest was an accurate portrayal of the success of big businesses, as the average citizen was at such a disadvantage socially and financially. They believed that survival of the wealthy would be a more accurate description and called for wealth to be equally distributed in society.

# John D. Rockefeller

Andrew Carnegie was not the only businessman to find a profit in oil wells. While Carnegie had invested in oil wells in Pennsylvania and Ohio, he did not make oil his primary business. A man who did decide to focus on oil was American industrialist John D. Rockefeller.

## A Career in Oil

John Davison Rockefeller was born in New York in 1839. His family relocated a couple of times within New York State before moving to Ohio in 1853. In 1859, Rockefeller left high school to take a business class at a local college and began working as an accountant. In 1863, he built his first oil refinery to process oil into usable products like fuel for transportation. Rockefeller believed that oil had a large future in America and decided to dedicate himself to the oil business. He formed the Standard Oil Company in 1870, which began to dominate the oil industry.

In 1881, Rockefeller established the Standard Oil Trust by forming an agreement in which his largest competitors were placed under the control of nine trustees. Trustees are members of a board who have control and power over the business. Rockefeller was the head trustee. This was the first trust in the United States, which effectively eliminated Rockefeller's competition and gave him a monopoly over the oil industry. A monopoly is what happens when one business owner becomes the dominant supplier of a needed good. In Rockefeller's case, the good was oil. A businessman who holds a monopoly over an industry can get away with a lot, including increasing prices because they do not have to worry about competitors offering the goods at a lower price. Some states became concerned about

John D. Rockefeller Jr. continued his father's philanthropy with the creation of Rockefeller Center in 1933. Rockefeller Center continues to be a focus of art, entertainment, and culture in New York City.

monopolies and began to enact anti-monopoly laws to prevent future domination of industries by one company or person.

In 1890, the United States Congress passed the Sherman Antitrust Act. The act was passed to prevent monopolies from forming in an attempt to eliminate their competition. Rockefeller tried to get around anti-monopoly laws, but the Standard Oil Trust was found in violation of antitrust laws and was declared illegal. The trust, made up of over thirty companies, was then forced to dissolve.

## Rockefeller's Final Years and Lasting Influence

Carnegie and Rockefeller both profited greatly from industry in the late nineteenth century. They became two of the wealthiest men in the world. Following Carnegie's example, Rockefeller dedicated much of his later life to philanthropic causes. He retired at age fifty-six and dedicated the rest of his life to the founding of schools and institutions that could bring about positive changes for humanity. Rockefeller had five children with his wife, Laura. He and his son John D. Rockefeller Jr. founded institutes like Rockefeller University in 1901, which is dedicated to medical research and science studies, as well as the Rockefeller Foundation in 1913, with the intention of addressing human suffering in the world through medical research.

Rockefeller lived to be ninety-seven years old. He died in his home in 1937. After Rockefeller's death, his son continued the family legacy of philanthropy, helping to found the United Service Organization during World War II and providing funding for the arts through the Lincoln Center for the Performing Arts, Rockefeller Center, and the Museum of Modern Art.

# Reformers

In the late 1800s, reformers worked to change the way wealth was distributed throughout the country. A reformer is someone who is working to change something. In this case, they were trying to change the large gap between the poor and the wealthy. Wealthy businessmen like Carnegie, Morgan, and Rockefeller were often targets of their attacks and used as examples of the need for change. This is because reformers were concerned about businessmen like Carnegie and Rockefeller having a monopoly over their respective industries.

## Henry George

One nineteenth-century reformer was a man named Henry George. George felt that there was an uneven distribution of wealth in the United States. He did not think that it was right for someone to be as wealthy as Carnegie, Rockefeller, or Morgan while others in the country were very poor.

In 1879, George published *Progress and Poverty*, a book in which he argued that all taxes should be replaced with just one single tax. In it, he wrote of how society was being negatively affected by "making the land of a whole people the exclusive property of some."[1] George felt that it was unjust that landowners of large pieces of property could become extremely wealthy for doing nothing but owning land and charging others rent to live on it or use it. He thought that taxing land more heavily would be enough to keep landowners from becoming absurdly wealthy while so many others in the country continued to struggle in poverty. Though not made into law, George's "single-tax" movement did gain momentum in the United States.

## Edward Bellamy

Another reformer to argue for closing the gap between the poor and the wealthy was Edward Bellamy. Bellamy liked to use a metaphor to describe his views on social inequality in nineteenth-century society. He described the wealthy as passengers riding comfortably in a stagecoach, while the poor were the ones working to carry the stagecoach forward. Like Henry George, Bellamy also published a book in which he voiced his concerns about society and his vision for a future America. *Looking Backward, 2000–1887* envisions a future America where citizens are all equal, sharing in everything, with no one being considered greater or lesser than the other.

In it, Bellamy attacked capitalism, which had made businessmen like Carnegie very wealthy. Bellamy considered capitalism "stressful, oppressive, barbarous."[2] *Looking Backward* was published in 1888 and sold millions of copies to become a bestseller.

## Henry Demarest Lloyd

A third reformer during this time was Henry Demarest Lloyd. Lloyd also wrote a book expressing his views on capitalism and monopoly in the nineteenth century. His book, titled *Wealth Against Commonwealth*, was published in 1894. In it, Lloyd largely attacked Rockefeller's Standard Oil Company as well as laissez-faire. Laissez-faire meant letting business owners do as they wished and keeping the government from interfering in the workings of privately owned businesses. It was a popular policy among businessmen of the nineteenth century who did not want the government attempting to regulate their businesses. But Lloyd opposed it in his book, writing:

Our century, given to this *laissez-faire*—"leave the individual alone; he will do what is best for himself, and what is best for him is best for all"—has done one good: it has put society at the mercy of its own ideals, and has produced an actual anarchy in industry which is horrifying us into a change of doctrines ... The true *laissez-faire* is, let the individual do what the individual can do best, and let the community do what the community can do best.[3]

Lloyd felt that the big businesses were doing what was right for them and working only to better themselves rather than society as a whole.

# CHAPTER FOUR

# *Businessman and Author*

A ndrew Carnegie was known as a hard worker and a successful businessman. His business ventures were successful because he was strategic in business planning and resilient in overcoming obstacles. However, his work should not be summarized by his financial success alone. While his success in the steel industry should certainly be recognized, he was also accomplished and successful in other areas of his life. He achieved an education through his love of reading and was, in fact, mostly self-educated. He also authored many written works during his lifetime and spent his later years giving away all of the money he had earned.

Carnegie, seen here writing at his desk, wrote many works during his lifetime.

## A Strategic Businessman

Andrew Carnegie acknowledged during his lifetime how fortunate he believed he was in moving to America, and near the city of Pittsburgh specifically, during the mid-nineteenth century. Pittsburgh became a primary spot for the iron and steel industry to emerge and thrive due to its association with the railroad industry. Carnegie acknowledged that part of his success was the luck of moving to the right place at the right time. However, his success cannot be attributed to a convenient location alone. It was hard work, well-thought-out investments, and business strategies that truly earned Carnegie his brilliance as a businessman.

Carnegie was no stranger to hard labor, having worked since he arrived in America at age twelve. He endured years of physical labor before getting an opportunity to join the Pennsylvania Railroad in 1853. In his position at the railroad, he was able to learn the workings of the industry, make business connections, and understand how to handle important responsibilities. His experiences there provided him knowledge and hands-on business education that he was later able to apply to his own businesses. For example, he learned about accounting, about managing workers, and about financial investments.

Carnegie is responsible for recognizing the future of iron and steel in the United States in the late nineteenth century and for developing it into a thriving business. One of the reasons he was able to achieve such success was his business strategy of expanding when times were tough economically. Many businessmen in Carnegie's time started new ventures, building new plants and factories, when times were good economically. They considered starting a new business venture when the economy was struggling to be too much of a gamble and were afraid of losing their investment. Carnegie, however, chose to build new iron and steel plants when times were tough. His reasoning was that the materials he needed to build and expand would be cheaper. By building when materials cost less, he was able to make a larger profit once his new plants were up and running and producing iron and steel.

Carnegie also used a business strategy called vertical integration, in which he purchased the businesses necessary to keep his own business operating. For his steel business, he would purchase anything necessary to his production. He purchased coal and iron mines and the railroad companies. He needed coal and iron to make steel, and since he owned the mines, he could keep his costs down. He could also ensure sales and eliminate competition by purchasing and controlling companies that were large customers of his, such as railroads. Vertical integration is now considered a form of monopoly and is illegal. However, in Carnegie's day, there were no laws in place preventing him from controlling his own supplies and customers.

In the years during the Civil War, the price of iron went up and there was an issue with getting it delivered. Several railroads were involved in the war, transporting soldiers and supplies. When bridges burned due to battles or accidents, there were long interruptions in railroad service. Carnegie digested all of this information, and in a time when many others would not have dared to start a new business venture, Carnegie decided to form his own rail-making company. He saw the demand for railroads and lasting bridges and knew that if he could supply them, he could be very successful. It was with this business strategy in mind that Carnegie retired from his position at the Pennsylvania Railroad and formed the Keystone Bridge Company in 1865.

Carnegie was very strategic in applying his business knowledge and experience to the current state of the country and anticipating the country's next need. This strategic foresight helped him to recognize when the time was right to invest in sleeper cars for trains, oil, iron, and steel. He was handsomely rewarded when his business investments proved successful.

## Panic of 1873

In the late nineteenth century, many European investors were purchasing stock, or investing their money, in railroads. In 1873, the European stock market crashed, which means that the prices of their stocks suddenly dropped an enormous amount. European investors began selling off their stocks in American railroads. There was soon not enough money left invested in the railroads for them to be successful. Without any investors willing to finance them to build and expand, many railroads went bankrupt.

An American bank that was heavily invested in railroads at this time was Jay Cooke & Company in New York City. When the railroads went bankrupt, the bank did as well. This caused a great panic among the American people. They thought that if a bank as large as Jay Cooke & Company could fail, then their own banks could fail as well. They felt their money must not be safe in banks, and there were runs on banks across the country. A run is what happens when people rush to their banks in large crowds demanding to empty and close their accounts and receive their money in cash. This panic occurred nationwide, and at least one hundred banks failed and went bankrupt due to the national panic and large withdrawals of money. The bankruptcies placed the nation in an economic depression, or a period of declining economic activity when production and wages are low. Many businesses closed during the depression,

The Panic of 1873 caused financial institutions like banks and the New York Stock Exchange to close their doors on customers, as depicted in this illustration.

as they saw less demand for their products and were making less money. The depression lasted until 1879.

During the depression, when smaller businesses were closing, larger companies like Carnegie's were sometimes considered more valuable. Carnegie had a lot of capital, or money, invested in his business. As smaller iron businesses closed, people turned to Carnegie to fulfill their iron needs. He was able to use this time period as an opportunity to expand his business, as some of his competition did not have the capital or productivity to continue to compete with him. However, this period of time was not without stress or anxiety for Carnegie. He had been vacationing in his summer home in the Alleghany Mountains when he received a telegram stating that the Jay Cooke & Company bank had gone bankrupt. In his autobiography, Carnegie referred to the Panic of 1873 as "the most anxious period of my business life."[1] He was less anxious about paying his company's bills than he was about receiving payments from his customers. But his company produced a strong profit each year, and neither Carnegie nor his business partners lived luxuriously or spent money extravagantly. Carnegie felt confident that they could ride out the depression, which they ultimately did.

Another business strategy that Carnegie employed was embracing new technology and inventions that could make his plants more productive, producing more product at a reduced cost. Around 1873, Carnegie visited Englishman Henry Bessemer. Bessemer had invented a way to turn iron into steel. He called this the Bessemer process. Carnegie believed that steel was superior to iron, but it was very expensive to make.

While initially skeptical of the Bessemer process, Carnegie ultimately embraced it after his meeting with Bessemer. It was his willingness to try this new technology and envision a future for steel in America that led Carnegie to his greatest financial success, the formation of Carnegie Steel. Carnegie's willingness to try the new Bessemer process and look toward the future of the iron and steel industry during the Panic

# THE BESSEMER PROCESS

In the mid-1800s, iron was a thriving business throughout the world. The invention of the railroad had created a high demand for iron. Cast iron was very hard, but it was also brittle, carrying the risk of breaking easily. Wrought iron was tougher than cast iron but was also a softer metal. It was well known to those in the industry that steel was a superior metal to build with than iron, but it was very expensive to manufacture.

In the late 1840s, American William Kelly began experimenting with a process that would remove impurities from iron in its most raw form. Through the use of an air blast, or a powerful burst of air through a furnace, he was able to alter the iron and turn it into steel. In 1856, Englishman Henry Bessemer had been working on the same idea, made the same discoveries as Kelly had, and patented his process. Kelly did not have the financial resources that Bessemer did to develop and market this new process. Thus, the Bessemer process was born and became a huge success.

After the Bessemer process was invented, a Swedish man named Goran Goransson improved upon it by redesigning the furnace. Goransson was able to make the furnace and the process more reliable, which resulted in the ability to mass-produce steel as it had never been produced before.

The Bessemer process revolutionized the iron and steel industry in America and Britain. Steel began to replace iron in the construction of bridges and railroads.

of 1873 and the ensuing depression is another example of Carnegie progressing his business forward during uncertain economic times.

## Overcoming Obstacles

No businessman may be successful without being able to address and overcome the unexpected. There were many obstacles that Carnegie faced throughout this career, including strikes and unfavorable public opinion. Carnegie had to learn to be a problem solver in order to continue to advance his career and business.

### The Homestead Strike

Perhaps the largest stain on Carnegie's career and reputation was the Homestead Strike. Carnegie faced backlash from the public after the violent eruption between workers and security guards at his Homestead steel mill in 1892. Some people accused Carnegie of being cowardly for remaining in Scotland during the strike instead of returning to America to address the issue and support his business partners, particularly Henry Clay Frick. However, others came to Carnegie's defense, stating that his business partners did not want him to return to America right away because of his tendency to give in to worker demands.

Carnegie felt redeemed after holding a large meeting in Pittsburgh with his replacement mill workers and their wives. He recalled this meeting in his autobiography:

> I addressed them from both my head and my heart. The one sentence I remember, and always shall, was to the effect that capital, labor, and employer were a three-legged stool, none before or after the others, all equally indispensable. Then came the cordial hand-

shaking and all was well. Having thus rejoined hands and hearts with our employees and their wives, I felt that a great weight had been effectually lifted.[2]

From that time on, he considered the issue resolved and hoped that public and worker opinions around his lack of presence during the Homestead Strike had been settled.

## Robber Baron

Robber barons were cruel businessmen who used ruthless business practices to get ahead and showed no compassion for others, including the working class. Many successful industrialists in the nineteenth century were thought of as robber barons, including John D. Rockefeller, J. P. Morgan, and Carnegie.

Carnegie was conscious of the public's opinion of himself. It was distressing to him to be thought of as a robber baron. Many people during this time period considered big businesses and their owners to be corrupt. It was thought that "the energetic search for wealth led to corrupt business practices such as stock manipulation, bribery, and cutthroat competition."[3]

Carnegie's defense against the accusation of being a robber baron was to respond through words and actions. Robber barons were depicted as greedy individuals who were only interested in bettering themselves. In his book *The Gospel of Wealth*, Carnegie stated his belief in the exact opposite. He stated that the wealthy had an obligation to help the less fortunate and called on fellow millionaires to give away their fortunes. Ultimately, the goal of a robber baron is to become a monopoly and completely dominate an industry. Though he eventually monopolized the steel industry, Carnegie was not in favor of monopolies. He also addressed competition in *The Gospel of Wealth*:

The price which society pays for the law of competition, like the price it pays for cheap comforts and luxuries, is also great; but the advantages of this law are also greater still, for it is to this law that we owe our wonderful material development, which brings improved conditions in its train.[4]

Carnegie was stating that it was competition, not monopoly, which brought about improved conditions for workers and society as a whole. He also acknowledged that it was laws in place at the time, such as anti-monopoly laws, that made industry growth and competition possible.

Unable to change the public's view of him as a robber baron through words alone, Carnegie turned toward taking

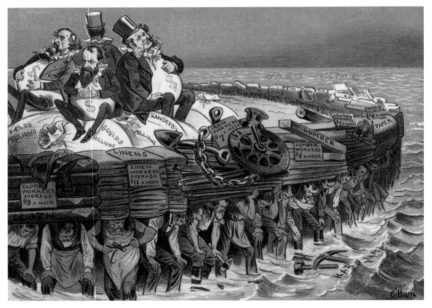

This cartoon shows wealthy businessmen as robber barons. The businessmen prosper at the expense of workers, who endure hard labor and poor conditions to keep factories and plants running.

action. Although he was accused of being a cruel and ruthless businessman, Carnegie did keep his word, and upon retirement, he donated most of his fortune to philanthropic causes.

## Writings

Carnegie wrote a lot during his lifetime. His written works not only showcased his success as a businessman but also his success as a learned man. Carnegie was largely self-educated. With little formal education, it is a testament to his willingness and determination to learn that he was able to write such a large number of works that were so well received.

### Triumphant Democracy

In 1886, Carnegie published *Triumphant Democracy; or, Fifty Years' March of the Republic*, a book dedicated to the greatness of America, particularly America's democracy and capitalism. America had fulfilled the promise of prosperity that the Carnegie family had sought when they immigrated in the nineteenth century. Carnegie desired to point out to Britain that many of their economic and societal problems, he believed, could be solved by following America's example. Carnegie felt that America was leading the world and praised the country in his book as "a strong yet free government ... where education is every man's birthright, where higher rewards are offered to labor and enterprise than elsewhere, and where the equality of political rights is secured."[5]

### The Gospel of Wealth

One of Carnegie's most well-known books was *The Gospel of Wealth*. It was originally published as an essay in the *North American Review* literary magazine in 1889 and later published in book form in 1900. *The Gospel of Wealth* detailed Carnegie's views on wealth and the responsibilities that he believed accompanied great wealth. In *The Gospel of Wealth*, Carnegie stated that "the problem of our age is the proper administration of wealth, so that the ties of brotherhood may still bind together the rich and poor in harmonious relationship."[6]

Throughout his lifetime, Carnegie never forgot the message his father proclaimed during Carnegie's childhood in Scotland, that citizens should be considered and treated equally, that the wealthy should not live in luxury while others struggle to survive. It is this sentiment that Carnegie expresses in *The Gospel of Wealth*, which made it a guiding resource for the field of philanthropy.

## Autobiography

Carnegie kept notes and memoirs of his travels with friends throughout his adult life. Prior to his death, he had been working on a series of memoirs that he had planned to publish as his autobiography. Then World War I broke out in 1914, and Carnegie stopped writing. After his death in 1919, his widow decided to pursue publication of his autobiography. She had the following to say about her late husband's writing:

> For a few weeks each summer we retired to our little bungalow on the moors at Aultnagar [the Carnegies' hunting lodge in Scotland] to enjoy the simple life, and it was there that Mr. Carnegie did most of his writing. He delighted in going back to those early times, and as he wrote he lived them all over again. He was thus engaged in July, 1914, when the war clouds began to gather, and when the fateful news of the 4th of August reached us, we immediately left

our retreat in the hills and returned to Skibo to be more in touch with the situation.

These memoirs ended at that time. Henceforth he was never able to interest himself in private affairs. Many times he made the attempt to continue writing, but found it useless ... Written with his own hand on the fly-leaf of his manuscript are these words: "It is probable that material for a small volume might be collected from these memoirs which the public would care to read, and that a private and larger volume might please my relatives and friends. Much I have written from time to time may, I think, wisely be omitted. Whoever arranges these notes should be careful not to burden the public with too much. A man with a heart as well as a head should be chosen."[7]

The fact that Carnegie's life ended on such a sad note was troubling to many who knew him. He had been known by many, including his widow, as a cheerful man. But as a pacifist and a promoter of peace, his spirit was deeply wounded when World War I began. As he had expressed his desire while alive to publish his writings, Louise Carnegie honored his wish and published his autobiography in 1920.

# CHAPTER FIVE

⌒

# *Responses to Carnegie's Career and Works*

S uccess in any industry is not achievable without motivation. Andrew Carnegie's motivation for success remained the same in his childhood jobs as it did in his later career as a steel tycoon. He desired to provide for his family and those less fortunate than himself. Carnegie was not motivated by greed or a desire to live in luxury, despite accusations of corrupt business practices. While he lived comfortably, he longed for when he could retire and spend his days distributing his fortune. But what was the public's response to Carnegie's motivation and his works? Were his business successes, written works, and philanthropy embraced by them?

Carnegie, seen here around 1900, endured praise as well as much criticism for his works.

## Response to Business Practices

Reformers such as Henry George, Edward Bellamy, and Henry Demarest Lloyd were not the only critics Carnegie had to contend with during this career. It was a strong desire to change society that fueled reformers like them and ushered in the Progressive Era. The Progressive Era took place in the United States between the 1890s and the 1920s, and was a time of intense reform when people sought to eliminate the corrupt practices of big businesses. Often considered one of the corrupt businessmen of this time, Carnegie had to contend with reformers and muckrakers who did not respond well to his success. Muckrakers were journalists and novelists who wrote books during the Progressive Era in an attempt to expose corrupt businessmen, including Carnegie. They were some of the first investigative journalists, and many of them were women.

The term "muckraker" was coined by Theodore Roosevelt when he referred to the actions of the journalists and novelists as raking the "muck," or stirring up and exposing the corrupt practices in the government and in big businesses. Muckrakers were highly critical of Carnegie's wealth, particularly at the expense of the working class.

In 1903, Carnegie was exposed by one muckraker in particular named James Howard Bridge. Bridge had been Carnegie's assistant for a number of years and had helped Carnegie write his book *Triumphant Democracy*. Having worked closely with Carnegie for a long time, Bridge had exclusive, firsthand knowledge about Carnegie Steel and Carnegie's business dealings. In 1903, Bridge published a book titled *The Inside History of the Carnegie Steel Company: A Romance of Millions*. Bridge's book exposed the inner workings of the steel company and the relationship between Carnegie and Henry

Clay Frick. Their connection had been strained ever since the Homestead Strike of 1892. In his book, Bridge revealed arguments and harsh words that he had heard exchanged between the two men in one of their last conversations before Carnegie sold the steel company to J. P. Morgan and retired.

Bridge's book created quite a stir when it was published and received mixed reviews. It was viewed by some as an insider's account of the business and taken as fact, while others questioned the accuracy of Bridge's memories and claims. Others reprimanded him for sharing anything that may have been confidential information obtained while working for Carnegie.

As a result of the Progressive Era and the efforts of the muckrakers, more labor unions began forming to protect workers' rights and to ensure acceptable wage compensation and safe and healthy working environments.

## Response to Written Works

Carnegie authored several essays, letters, speeches, memoirs, and books throughout his life, drawing on his own experiences and his own observations since arriving in America. His written works were largely well received and some, such as his autobiography, remain in print today.

### Reception of *Triumphant Democracy*

Having experienced success in America, Carnegie felt compelled to write about the greatness of the country in his book *Triumphant Democracy*. He felt that he had a special appreciation for America because he was not born in the country. In fact, Carnegie felt that those who were natural-born American citizens could not appreciate the country in the way he could. When he published *Triumphant Democracy*, he wrote the following dedication:

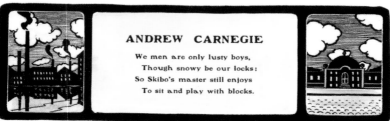

**ANDREW CARNEGIE**

We men are only lusty boys,
  Though snowy be our locks;
So Skibo's master still enjoys
  To sit and play with blocks.

This cartoon from 1903 depicts Carnegie in a childish position building libraries. The cartoon makes fun of Carnegie, portraying him playing with money like children play with blocks.

To the BELOVED REPUBLIC under whose equal laws I am made the peer of any man, although denied political equality by my native land, I DEDICATE THIS BOOK with an intensity of gratitude and admiration which the native-born citizen can neither feel nor understand.[1]

While Carnegie's book was well received, selling over seventy thousand copies, there were some who were critical of Carnegie's cheery disposition. One critic felt that Carnegie romanticized his writings and his musings about the greatness of America. He referred to *Triumphant Democracy* as "sunshine, sunshine, sunshine."[2] Whether this reader felt that Carnegie had too cheery of a disposition or whether he felt that Carnegie's musings were skewed by his wealth is unknown. Those close to him knew Carnegie as a man with a generally cheerful outlook on life, and he chose to dismiss this kind of criticism rather than take it as a personal insult.

## Reception of *The Gospel of Wealth*

Carnegie's written works were generally well received by the public, particularly his essay "Wealth," published in 1889 and later in 1900 as the more well-known book *The Gospel of Wealth*. His ideas about the wealthy giving back to those less fortunate struck a chord with the public, who found Carnegie's philanthropy inspiring. But Carnegie was also met with criticism. Some were confused upon its release since Carnegie, one of the wealthiest men in the world, was openly criticizing his own class. Others were openly critical of his work, particularly in regards to his belief in survival of the fittest. In *The Gospel of Wealth*, Carnegie wrote of his commitment to social Darwinism:

While the law may be sometimes hard for the individual, it is best for the race, because it insures the survival of the fittest in every department. We accept and welcome therefore, as conditions to which we must accommodate ourselves, great inequality of environment, the concentration of business, industrial and commercial, in the hands of a few, and the law of competition between these, as being not only beneficial, but essential for the future progress of the race.[3]

This passage was a particular source of controversy. Carnegie's reference to the survival of the fittest was interpreted by some as stating that the wealthy were stronger and more skilled, or the "fittest," and thus were the ones who had achieved such great success. Carnegie's idea of the wealthy "fittest" giving away their fortunes, designating where money should go, was thought to imply that Carnegie viewed the wealthy as more capable and competent in decision making than those in the working class.

Drawing further criticism was a passage in which Carnegie referred to the wealthy man as superior and more intelligent when it came to determining how to distribute funds:

This, then, is held to be the duty of the man of Wealth: First, to set an example of modest, unostentatious living, shunning display or extravagance; to provide moderately for the legitimate wants of those dependent upon him; and after doing so to consider all surplus revenues which come to him simply as trust funds, which he is called upon to administer, and strictly bound as a matter of duty to administer in the manner which, in his judgment, is best calculated to produce the most beneficial results for the community—the man of wealth thus becoming the mere agent and trustee for his poorer brethren, bringing to their service his superior wisdom, experience and ability to administer, doing for them better than they would or could do for themselves.[4]

Some of the working class were offended by Carnegie's implications that they could not determine for themselves how charitable funds should best be used. Many joined together to protest Carnegie, telling people not to accept his financial gifts and to boycott his free libraries.

Carnegie received further criticism for his listing of the various fields of philanthropy to which the wealthy should distribute their funds. He listed them in what he believed was the order of importance: universities, free libraries, hospitals and institutions dedicated to relieving human illness and suffering, parks, halls for meetings and concerts, indoor swimming baths or indoor swimming pools, and church buildings. Many people were outraged over Carnegie's list, including ministers and church organizations. They were furious to find churches at the bottom of Carnegie's list—even after swimming pools. Also upset were artists and musicians, who did not appreciate being left out and felt that some money should be dedicated to their fields as well. Private schools, orphanages, and charities all felt snubbed and offered public criticisms of Carnegie's message.

The largest critic of *The Gospel of Wealth* was a man named William Jewett Tucker. Tucker was a theologian, meaning he studied religion and God. In 1891, he published a harsh critique of *The Gospel of Wealth* in the *Andover Review*, a popular religious magazine. In his critique, Tucker attacked Carnegie's

$100,000,000
GIVEN FOR
THE PUBLIC
GOOD
CANADA
N. DAKOTA
S. DAKOTA
NEB
MINN.
IOWA
WIS
ILLINOIS
INDIANA
OHIO
PENN.
KENTUCKY
W. VIRGINIA
VIRGINIA
TENNESSEE.
NORTH CAROLINA.
ALA
LIBRARY
Dalrymple
COPYRIGHT 1903 BY JUDGE COMPANY OF NEW YORK.
TWO EXAMPLES FOR
The American by choice
N. Y. PUBLIC LIBRARY
PICTURE COLLECTION


This cartoon portrays Carnegie in Scottish clothing pouring money over the United States. It is intended to mock Carnegie for distributing his great wealth, often in the form of libraries.

theory that the proper distribution of wealth could bring about a balance and improvement to society. He stated that Carnegie was incorrect and that society's real problem was that such an enormous amount of wealth was in the hands of only a few people. The very wealthy were being allowed to dominate, or monopolize, industry and thus dominate society as well. Tucker did not agree that this would be resolved by the wealthy simply giving away their fortunes. He felt that they should never have been able to gain such fortunes to begin with while other citizens struggled financially just for survival.

Tucker also believed that the working class was capable of distributing and disposing of excess money or donations on their own, that they did not need a wealthy businessman to handle it for them. Tucker famously wrote in his critique: "I can conceive of no greater mistake, more disastrous in the end to religion if not to society, than that of trying to make charity do the work of justice."[5] Tucker meant that giving money away would not solve society's real problems but would only mask them. If the working class or poor received a large sum of money or charity, then it would initially appear that their lives and social status had improved. However, this would only be a temporary masking of the underlying issue of inequality. The wealthy few would continue to make more money while the many poor would remain poor. Tucker believed that the real issues of society needed to be addressed rather than glossed over with philanthropic gestures.

## Response to Philanthropy

It was in his retirement years that the public saw the side of Carnegie for which he is most well remembered today: his philanthropy. While most people embraced the message of philanthropy he put forth in *The Gospel of Wealth* and applauded the distribution of his wealth, there were some who were critical of his words and actions.

## Religious Objections

One of Carnegie's early philanthropic donations was that of a new organ to a church in Alleghany, Pennsylvania. Initially, the church had asked Carnegie for a financial contribution to replace their church building with a new building. But the congregation had less than one hundred members and Carnegie did not want to donate a large amount of money to such a small congregation. However, he was still willing to help in some way. He donated the new organ instead.

Word quickly spread of Carnegie's donation to the church, and other churches were soon requesting that he provide new organs for their churches too. So many churches were putting in requests that Carnegie eventually developed a system for church organ donations, including an application and a donation schedule. The churches were pleased that Carnegie was being so generous with his funds.

Not everyone was happy about Carnegie's donations of organs to the churches, though. The Scottish Highlands, a mountainous area in northwest Scotland, had some very strict Christian residents. The Presbyterians in particular believed in worshipping at church using their God-given voices only and no musical instruments. When word of Carnegie's donations of church organs reached the Scottish Highlands, some residents there denounced Carnegie and accused him of demoralizing Christian worship. Carnegie recalled these accusations in his autobiography. He stated that he had personally experienced music during worship at church to be beneficial. He defended his actions, stating, "I feel the money spent for organs is well spent. So we continue the organ department."[6]

By 1919, the organs Carnegie had donated totaled over seven thousand and cost him over $6 million (over $84 million in 2018).

## Response to Libraries

Carnegie openly admitted that libraries were the top philanthropic priority for him. Since his boyhood, Carnegie had delighted in reading and believed that libraries and books illuminated the mind in a way nothing else could. He eventually developed design templates for his libraries and sometimes requested that a rising sun be engraved near the entrance to the libraries to symbolize the illumination they offered.

His first gift of a public library was given in his hometown of Dunfermline, Scotland, on August 29, 1883. He went on to open thousands of libraries all over the world, including in the United States, the United Kingdom, Australia, and New Zealand.

While his libraries offered a great resource to many communities, there were some who were critical of his donations. Some people believed that Carnegie's motivation for his donations came less from a true spirit of philanthropy and more from a desire to repair his image in the eyes of many who had thought him a corrupt businessman for years. In one instance, Carnegie's offer to fund a library in Louisville, Kentucky, was met with a stern rebuttal from the city. An article in a Louisville paper declared the city's willingness to accept and maintain a library, but its utter disinterest in building a monument to Carnegie. Others argued that Carnegie should

# THE POWER OF THE PEN

One of Carnegie's earliest works was an anonymous letter he wrote to a newspaper as a boy. After coming to America with his family, Carnegie enjoyed a local library in Pittsburgh. It was made available to the community by a local man named Colonel James Anderson. Since Carnegie was unable to afford books of his own to read, the library was an invaluable resource to him. He described the library as "a blessing from above, a means by which the treasures of literature were unfolded to me."[7] At the time, Carnegie was working as a telegraph messenger boy and was dismayed when he learned that the library was only available to "working boys," or boys who did physical labor with their hands. Messenger boys and clerks were not permitted to use the library. Undeterred, Carnegie wrote an anonymous letter to a local Pittsburgh newspaper, stating that he believed that the library should be open to all boys. He signed the letter "Working Boy," and after some back and forth correspondence in the newspaper, Colonel Anderson opened his library to all boys. Carnegie later recalled in his autobiography the experience of having the library opened:

> In this way the windows were opened in the walls of my dungeon through which the light of knowledge streamed in. Every day's toil and even the long hours of night service were lightened by the book which I carried about with me and read in the intervals that could be snatched from duty. And the future was made bright by the thought that when Saturday came a new volume could be obtained.[8]

Carnegie took away from this experience a lesson about the power of the written word that would stay with him the rest of his life. This experience also heavily influenced his philanthropic donations to libraries in his later life.

Carnegie had a lifelong love of reading, and can be seen here enjoying a magazine at home.

have distributed his wealth among his many employees rather than donating to outside communities.

## Contemporary Response to Carnegie's Work

Inspired by Andrew Carnegie's generous financial gifts, philanthropy grew into a popular movement in the twentieth and twenty-first centuries, with millionaires making large donations to hospitals, education, and scientific research. This philanthropic movement continues today and can be traced back over one hundred years to Andrew Carnegie, the publication of *The Gospel of Wealth*, and the way he led by example through giving away his fortune. Carnegie remains an influence to successful businessmen and businesswomen who choose to give away large sums of their fortunes. In contemporary philanthropic circles, Carnegie is revered and often referred to as the most influential philanthropist in American history.

An example of a contemporary philanthropist who has followed Carnegie's example is Bill Gates. Bill Gates is the founder of the Microsoft Corporation. He has been compared to Andrew Carnegie, as they both achieved great financial success and have both donated large sums of money to charitable causes. Gates has stated that he has found inspiration in Carnegie, whom he credits as one of the first big philanthropists. To date, Gates has given away over $1 billion of his fortune to philanthropic causes.

Another example of a modern-day Carnegie is Warren Buffett. Just as Carnegie had success with his financial investments, Warren Buffett has also achieved great success as an investor. Inspired by Carnegie's *The Gospel of Wealth*, Warren Buffett, with Bill Gates and Gates's wife Melinda, created a "Giving Pledge" in 2010. The "Giving Pledge" is a call for the

Bill and Melinda Gates, seen here in 2017, have followed Carnegie's philanthropic example and have given away over $1 billion to charitable causes.

wealthiest Americans to commit to giving away more than half their wealth. The movement quickly spread outside the United States as willing millionaires and billionaires took interest and took the pledge. The pledge is reminiscent of the letter Carnegie wrote to himself as a young businessman, vowing to retire and give away his fortune. It shows that Carnegie's philanthropic endeavors and *The Gospel of Wealth* are still providing inspiration to philanthropists today.

# CHAPTER SIX

# Carnegie's Lasting Legacy

In 1868, Andrew Carnegie wrote a letter to himself pledging to retire from business at age thirty-five. A multimillionaire, Carnegie wanted to live on $50,000 a year and distribute the rest of his fortune to philanthropic causes. While Carnegie did not retire until he was in his sixties, he did dedicate his retirement to giving away his fortune. He made millions of dollars in donations toward causes that he believed would benefit mankind. Several of the institutions Carnegie opened with his immense wealth are still in existence today, including libraries, schools, trusts, museums, and facilities dedicated to the arts.

Carnegie is seen here around 1910 at his estate during his retirement years.

# Libraries

When Carnegie was a child living in Scotland with his family, his father, William, and several neighborhood men pooled their books together so they could loan them out to their neighbors who did not have books and could not afford to purchase any. They had created a free local library for their community.

William's actions were an inspiration to his son, and his appreciation of libraries became more apparent as he grew more successful in his career. Carnegie began opening public libraries, starting with his first in Dunfermline, his boyhood home, on August 29, 1883. Carnegie's mother, Margaret, had laid the first stone on July 27, 1881. Since William Carnegie had died years earlier, it meant a great deal to Carnegie to have his mother present for the laying of the library's foundation in their hometown. As the library's creator, Carnegie provided funds so that it could be stocked with books and to help with the maintenance of the building.

Carnegie felt that there was "no use to which money could be applied so productive of good to boys and girls who have good within them and ability and ambition to develop it, as the founding of a public library."[1] When Carnegie wrote this passage in his autobiography, he was recollecting his own memories of gratitude at being able to use the library of Colonel James Anderson in Western Pennsylvania as a young boy. Carnegie believed throughout his life that providing children who were eager to learn with a means through which they could learn, like a free library, was one of the greatest gifts he could give.

Carnegie also opened libraries in the United States. Returning to his adopted home of Pittsburgh, where he had achieved so much success since immigrating to America,

Many Carnegie libraries are still open and in use today, such as this one in Bryan, Texas.

Carnegie donated $1 million to build the Carnegie Library of Pittsburgh. The library was a network of seven branches, or individual library buildings, throughout the city of Pittsburgh. The branches were built over a ten-year period, with the first branch opening in 1898 and the last branch opening in 1908. Throughout his life, Carnegie opened over 2,500 libraries all over the world, many of which are still open and in use today.

# Carnegie-Mellon University

Once again returning to his adopted hometown of Pittsburgh, in 1900, Carnegie made a $1 million donation to build a technical institute, called Carnegie Technical Schools. Carnegie was concerned about the working class's ability to increase their skillset and advance their careers. He wanted a school dedicated to the working class, where they could improve their skills and learn new trades. At Carnegie Technical Schools, one could earn a two- or three-year certificate in the arts or in engineering. Included in the technical school was a college for women. It was named the Margaret Morrison Carnegie College, in honor of Andrew Carnegie's mother. In 1912, Carnegie Technical Schools was renamed Carnegie Institute of Technology. This college is still in existence today as part of Carnegie-Mellon University.

Near to the Carnegie Technical Schools was a science research center called the Mellon Institute. It was named after the Mellon family of Pittsburgh. The Mellons, like the Carnegies, had immigrated to America in the nineteenth century and achieved great financial success. In 1967, the two institutes merged, forming Carnegie-Mellon University. The university continues to enroll new students today.

# Carnegie Hall

Throughout his adult life, Carnegie enjoyed and supported the arts. He took a special interest after marrying his wife, Louise. She was a subscriber of the Oratorio Society of New York, a choral group, and enjoyed attending their concerts. In 1884, Carnegie joined the society's board of directors. For years, the society had desired to build a hall suitable for their choral performances. In 1887, they got that chance when Carnegie supported their concert hall fund.

Two years later, Carnegie had organized the concert hall, called the Music Hall Company of New York. He was the main financial contributor to the project, donating over $1 million (over $27 million in 2018). The music hall opened on May 5, 1891, and over the years featured international musical artists such as Russian composer Pyotr Ilyich Tchaikovsky and Polish pianist Ignacy Jan Paderewski. Paderewski made his American debut at the hall.

While Carnegie was initially reluctant to attach his name to the music hall, he was convinced by the controlling board in 1893 to let them rename the company Carnegie Hall. Carnegie had wanted the music hall to be associated with music and the arts first and not the Carnegie name. But due to Carnegie's financial backing, many people already referred to it as Carnegie's Hall. Carnegie Hall is still open today, welcoming musical artists from all over the world.

## Carnegie Institution for Science

In 1901, Carnegie decided that he would like to open an institute dedicated to scientific knowledge and research. He approached then president of the United States Theodore Roosevelt and offered $10 million (over $294 million in 2018) to fund the project. Over the next decade, Carnegie would donate an additional $12 million (over $315 million in 2018). In 1903, Congress incorporated the institute, making it a legal corporation. This means that the institute was able to legally conduct business. Initially named the Carnegie Institute of Washington, the institute was renamed the Carnegie Institution for Science in 2007.

Carnegie Hall, seen here, has become synonymous with great musical talent. Musicians and entertainers from all over the world come to Carnegie Hall to showcase their skills and provide entertainment.

The institute has hosted many researchers and famous scientists over the years who have made important discoveries. One scientist was Edwin Hubble, who discovered that there are other galaxies besides our own Milky Way galaxy in our expanding universe. The Hubble Telescope, a very large and powerful telescope, was named after Hubble due to his contributions to space study. Another was Charles Richter, who created the Richter scale, a way to measure the size and power of earthquakes. A third scientist was Vera Rubin, who proved that dark matter exists in our universe. Rubin was awarded the National Medal of Science for her groundbreaking discovery. The Carnegie Institution for Science still exists and is headquartered in Washington, DC.

## The Carnegie Hero Fund Commission

As a pacifist, Andrew Carnegie believed in nonviolent conflict resolution. He believed in being peaceful with one another and in helping others. One of Carnegie's philanthropic undertakings was to set up a fund, or financial account, dedicated to rewarding individuals who performed heroic acts. Carnegie also wanted the fund to offer financial support to the individuals and families who were left behind when someone died in a heroic act.

When his father died, young Carnegie became the head of the household and took on the responsibility of providing for his family. His mother assisted as best she could, but the Carnegies continued to struggle financially until Carnegie achieved financial success in investments and business. Having personally experienced the struggles of a family that had lost their main financial supporter, Carnegie wanted to assist others who were enduring the same thing, particularly

In keeping with Carnegie's nonviolent nature, the Carnegie Medal, seen here, is awarded four times a year to civilians who have demonstrated great bravery and kindness toward fellow citizens.

if a family had lost the head of their household in an act of heroism. In his Deed of Trust for his Hero Fund Commission, Carnegie stated:

Gentlemen: We live in a heroic age. Not seldom are we thrilled by deeds of heroism where men or women are injured or lose their lives in attempting to preserve or rescue their fellows; such the heroes of civilization. I have long felt that the heroes and those dependent upon them should be freed from pecuniary cares resulting from their heroism.[2]

The Carnegie Hero Fund Commission was created in 1904 and still offers awards and financial assistance today. One of the most recognizable symbols of the commission is the Carnegie Medal. The commission itself outlines the following qualifications to receive the Carnegie Medal and qualify for financial assistance:

> The candidate for an award must be a civilian who voluntarily risks his or her life to an extraordinary degree while saving or attempting to save the life of another person. The rescuer must have no full measure of responsibility for the safety of the victim. There must be conclusive evidence to support the act's occurrence, and the act must be called to the attention of the Commission within two years.
>
> Those who are selected for recognition by the Commission are awarded the CARNEGIE MEDAL, and they, or their survivors, become eligible for financial considerations, including one-time grants, scholarship aid, death benefits, and continuing assistance.[3]

Since the Carnegie Hero Fund Commission started, tens of thousands of nominations have been received and thousands of Carnegie Medals have been awarded. Some medals are given after the nominees have died in a heroic act, while other nominees are still living upon receiving the award. Carnegie Medals are awarded four times each year.

## Carnegie Museums of Pittsburgh

Throughout his life, Carnegie had an appreciation for literary arts. He loved books and reading, as evidenced by his generous donations of libraries. However, Carnegie also had an appreciation of music and art, and a great respect for scientific research. In 1895, he established the Carnegie Museums of Pittsburgh. Carnegie invested $20 million in building the original structure. It has since grown into multiple buildings, including a library, art gallery, music hall, and museum of natural history. The natural history museum has two dinosaurs on display, aptly named *Diplodocus carnegie* and *Apatosaurus louisae*, in honor of Carnegie and his wife, Louise.

Today, the Carnegie Museums of Pittsburgh continue Carnegie's mission toward arts and science-based education. They are popular places for educational field trips and welcome more than four hundred thousand schoolchildren each year.

## Carnegie Corporation of New York

By the time he reached his seventies, Carnegie had spent a large portion of his fortune in philanthropic endeavors. But he still had not been able to give his entire fortune away as he had hoped and planned. In 1911, he created the Carnegie Corporation of New York, through which he hoped to give away the remainder of his wealth, approximately $150 million (over $3 billion in 2018). The Carnegie Corporation of New York is a philanthropic foundation that supports four main areas: education, democracy, international peace and security, and higher education and research in Africa. It exists today, offering large grants, or large sums of money dedicated to a specific purpose, to various educational institutes, such as schools, universities, and colleges.

# CARNEGIE
# DUNFERMLINE TRUST

While many of Andrew Carnegie's philanthropic endeavors benefited the United States, specifically the cities of Pittsburgh and New York, Carnegie never forgot where he came from. A proud Scotsman, Carnegie made sure to distribute part of his fortune in his home country. In 1903, he turned his attention to his hometown, Dunfermline, where he established the Carnegie Dunfermline Trust. Carnegie donated approximately $4 million (over $108 million in 2018) to benefit Dunfermline's citizens. Through this trust, the residents received many benefits, including new parks and playing fields, reading rooms, schools, a music institute, a women's center, and a youth center.

While distributing his wealth, Carnegie remembered his humble beginnings in his hometown of Dunfermline, Scotland, seen here.

## US Steel

Carnegie's legacy in the steel industry of the nineteenth century is not forgotten in the steel industry of today. When J. P. Morgan purchased Carnegie Steel in 1901, he formed the United States Steel Corporation, or US Steel. Keeping Carnegie's legacy alive, US Steel conducts business today in what they refer to as "the Carnegie Way."[4] The US Steel website describes their business method:

> The Carnegie Way looks at all aspects of our business to find ways we can improve. That includes processes, products and our culture. Started in 2013, it provides employees with a structured way to identify solutions that create value, drive innovation and ignite change. The Carnegie Way is moving us in the right direction.[5]

US Steel is still a leading supplier of steel, and true to Carnegie's roots, it is headquartered in Pittsburgh, Pennsylvania.

# CHRONOLOGY

**1825** The Erie Canal is completed.

**1835** Andrew Carnegie is born in Dunfermline, Scotland.

**1845** Frederick Douglass describes slave life in *Narrative of the Life of Frederick Douglass*.

**1846** The Pennsylvania legislature approves the Pennsylvania Railroad.

**1848** Carnegie comes to the United States with his family at age thirteen.

**1853** Carnegie takes a job at the Pennsylvania Railroad.

**1855** Carnegie's father, William Carnegie, dies.

**1861** Civil War begins and Carnegie works in the Transportation Department in Washington, DC.

**1862** Carnegie invests in an oil well in Pennsylvania

**1864** Carnegie is drafted by the Union army and pays a substitute to serve in his place.

**1865** Civil War ends and the Thirteenth Amendment to the US Constitution is ratified.

**1865** Carnegie forms the Keystone Bridge Company.

**1873** The Panic of 1873 and ensuing depression begins.

**1874** Carnegie opens Edgar Thomson Steel Works, his first steel plant.

**1883** The first Carnegie library opens in Dunfermline, Scotland.

**1885** Carnegie becomes a United States citizen.

**1889** Carnegie publishes his essay "Wealth," which later becomes the book *The Gospel of Wealth* (1900).

**1891** The Carnegie-funded Music Hall Company of New York opens.

**1892** Carnegie founds Carnegie Steel.

**1892** The Homestead Strike occurs at one of Carnegie's steel plants in Homestead, Pennsylvania.

**1901** Carnegie sells his business to the United States Steel Corporation.

**1914** World War I begins.

**1918** World War I ends.

**1919** Carnegie dies at one of his family estates in Massachusetts.

**1920** Carnegie's autobiography is published by his widow, Louise.

# GLOSSARY

**abolitionist** A person who worked to end slavery in the United States.

**Age of Reform** The period of time in the United States between 1830 and 1850 in which many movements were taking place to bring about changes to the country.

**Bessemer process** An affordable and revolutionary way to convert iron into steel, invented in the 1800s by Henry Bessemer.

**Civil War** A war fought in the United States between 1861 and 1865 after seven slave states seceded from the rest of the country to form the Confederate States of America.

**cotton gin** A machine created by Eli Whitney in 1793 that was used to separate cotton lint from cotton seeds.

**depression** A period of declining financial activity in which production and wages are low.

**Erie Canal** A large waterway that moved goods and passengers west from New York City and the Hudson River.

**immigration** When citizens leave their home countries to move to a different country.

**industrialist** Someone who creates and profits from machine-powered industry.

**Industrial Revolution** When machines were widely used to replace manual labor in the late 1700s and early 1800s, bringing factories and large economic growth to Britain and America.

**laissez-faire** When the government does not interfere with privately owned businesses.

**mechanization** When physical work traditionally done by hand is replaced by machines.

**monopoly** When one business owner becomes the dominant supplier of a needed good.

**Morse Code** A coding system invented by Samuel F. B. Morse in 1835 in which dots and dashes are used in place of numbers and letters.

**muckraker** Journalists and novelists who wrote books during the Progressive Era in an attempt to expose corrupt business practices.

**pacifism** A belief that violence is unnecessary and an unjustifiable means of solving disagreements.

**patriarchy** A society in which men are dominant.

**philanthropy** When one makes generous financial donations to others.

**Progressive Era** A period of intense reform in the United States between the 1890s and 1920s when people attempted to expose and eliminate corrupt businessmen.

**ratify** To formally adopt a change to the United States Constitution.

**reformer** One who works to bring about change.

**robber baron** A businessman who uses cruel business practices to be successful and shows no compassion for others.

**secede** To formally withdraw from something, such as a country.

**social Darwinism** When Charles Darwin's idea of survival of the fittest is applied to social relationships and business practices.

**strike** When a group of workers agrees to stop production as a form of protest.

**suffrage** The right to vote.

**telegraph** A way to send a message across a long distance using signals from an electric device and the dominant form of communication in the United States in the mid-1800s.

**Thirteenth Amendment** A change to the US Constitution in 1865 that made slavery illegal in the United States.

**trustee** A member of a group that has control and power over a business.

**workers' union** Organizations that exist to protect workers' rights.

**xenophobia** A fear of people from other countries.

# SOURCES

## CHAPTER ONE

1. "Primary Documents in American History: Louisiana Purchase," The Library of Congress, April 26, 0217, https://www.loc.gov/rr/program/bib/ourdocs/Louisiana.html.

2. Clare D. McGillem, "Telegraph," Encyclopedia Britannica, December 7, 2016, https://www.britannica.com/technology/telegraph.

3. Mark C. Carnes and John A. Garraty, *American Destiny Narrative of a Nation Volume I to 1877* (New York: Pearson Longman, 2006), 318.

4. Mark C. Carnes and John A. Garraty, *American Destiny Narrative of a Nation Volume I to 1877* (New York: Pearson Longman, 2006), 313.

## CHAPTER TWO

1. Andrew Carnegie, *The Autobiography of Andrew Carnegie* (Boston: Houghton Mifflin, 1920), 8.

2. Ibid., 9.

3. Ibid., 33.

4. Ibid., 76.

5. "Publications," Carnegie Corporation of New York, Accessed February 2, 2018, https://www.carnegie.org/publications/the-gospel-of-wealth.

# CHAPTER THREE

1. Henry George, *Progress and Poverty* (London, UK: William Reeves, 1884), 303.

2. Andrew Carnegie, *The Autobiography of Andrew Carnegie* (Boston, MA: Houghton Mifflin, 1920), xiv.

3. Henry Demarest Lloyd, *Wealth Against Commonwealth* (New York: Harper & Brothers Publishers, 1899), 496–497.

# CHAPTER FOUR

1. Andrew Carnegie, *The Autobiography of Andrew Carnegie* (Boston, MA: Houghton Mifflin, 1920), 182.

2. Ibid., 226.

3. Mark C. Carnes and John A. Garraty, *American Destiny Narrative of a Nation Volume II Since 1865* (New York: Pearson Longman, 2006), 503.

4. "About Our History: The Gospel of Wealth," Carnegie Corporation of New York, Accessed February 15, 2018, https://www.carnegie.org/about/our-history/gospelofwealth.

5. "Triumphant Democracy: US Railroads," Harvard University, Accessed February 15, 2018, https://www.library.hbs.edu/hc/railroads/us-railroads.html.

6. Ibid.

7. Andrew Carnegie, *The Autobiography of Andrew Carnegie* (Boston, MA: Houghton Mifflin, 1920), v-vi.

# CHAPTER FIVE

1. Andrew Carnegie, *Triumphant Democracy* (New York: J. J. Little & Co., 1886), dedication page.

2. Andrew Carnegie, *The Autobiography of Andrew Carnegie* (Boston, MA: Houghton Mifflin, 1920), xi.

3. "About Our History: The Gospel of Wealth," Carnegie Corporation of New York, Accessed February 15, 2018, https://www.carnegie.org/about/our-history/gospelofwealth.

4. Ibid.

5. Andrew Carnegie, *The Gospel of Wealth Essays and Other Writings*, (New York: Penguin Classics, 2006), iv.

6. Andrew Carnegie, *The Autobiography of Andrew Carnegie* (Boston, MA: Houghton Mifflin, 1920), 267–268.

7. Ibid., 43.

8. Ibid., 44.

# CHAPTER SIX

1. Andrew Carnegie, *The Autobiography of Andrew Carnegie* (Boston, MA: Houghton Mifflin, 1920), 45.

2. "Deed of Trust," Carnegie Hero Fund Commission, Accessed February 15, 2018, http://www.carnegiehero.org/deed-of-trust.

3. "Mission of the Carnegie Hero Fund Commission," Carnegie Hero Fund Commission, Accessed February 15, 2018, http://www.carnegiehero.org/about-the-fund/mission.

4. "About U.S. Steel," United States Steel Corporation, Accessed February 15, 2018, https://www.ussteel.com/about.

5. Ibid.

# FURTHER
# INFORMATION

## BOOKS

Colman, Penny. *Elizabeth Cady Stanton and Susan B. Anthony: A Friendship That Changed the World*. New York: Square Fish, 2016.

Douglass, Frederick. *Narrative of the Life of Frederick Douglass*. New Haven, CT: Yale University Press, 2016.

Hubbard, Ben. *Stories of Women During the Industrial Revolution: Changing Roles, Changing Lives*. London, UK: Heinemann, 2015.

Perelman, Dale Richard. *Steel: The Story of Pittsburgh's Iron and Steel Industry, 1852–1902*. New York: The History Press, 2016.

Springirth, Kenneth C. *Remembering the Pennsylvania Railroad*. America Through Time. Stroud, UK: Fonthill Media, LLC, 2015.

# WEBSITES

**Carnegie Corporation of New York**
https://www.carnegie.org/interactives/foundersstory

Learn about the foundation Andrew Carnegie formed before he died in the hopes of giving away the last of his fortune. Carnegie Corporation continues Andrew Carnegie's legacy of giving through furthering education, democracy, international peace and security, and higher education and research in Africa. There are sections on the website dedicated to these endeavors, as well as sections dedicated to learning more about Carnegie himself.

**Erie Canalway National Heritage Corridor**
https://eriecanalway.org/learn/history-culture

This website features a detailed history of the Erie Canal, including how it came to be built and the significant role it played during the nineteenth and early twentieth centuries.

**Library of Congress**
https://www.loc.gov

This website allows students to search for a range of topics in American history. They may learn more about the American Revolution, the Industrial Revolution, the Civil War, and the Thirteenth Amendment, to name a few.

# MUSEUMS

**Andrew Carnegie Mansion**
2 East 91st Street
New York, New York 10128

**Carnegie Science Center**
1 Allegheny Avenue
Pittsburgh, PA 15212
Carnegie Science Center

**Ellis Island National Museum of Immigration**
1 Liberty Island – Ellis Island
New York, NY 10004

# BIBLIOGRAPHY

"About the Society." Oratorio Society of New York. Accessed February 12, 2018. http://www.oratoriosocietyofny.org/about.php.

"An Age of Reform." *Encyclopedia Britannica*. Accessed February 2, 2018. https://www.britannica.com19/place/United-States/An-age-of-reform.

"Andrew Carnegie: The Richest Man in the World: Timeline: Rags to Riches." Public Broadcasting Service. Accessed February 14, 2018. http://www.pbs.org/wgbh/americanexperience/features/carnegie-timeline-rags-to-riches.

"Andrew Carnegie's Story: Giving and Legacy." Carnegie Corporation of New York. Accessed February 14, 2018. https://www.carnegie.org/interactives/foundersstory/#!/#giving-legacy.

Andrews, Evan. "Andrew Carnegie's Surprising Legacy." History.com. Last modified February 23, 2017. http://www.history.com/news/andrew-carnegies-surprising-legacy.

"The Annexation of Texas, the Mexican-American War, and the Treaty of Guadalupe-Hidalgo, 1845–1848." Office of the Historian. Accessed February 2, 2018. https://history.state.gov/milestones/1830-1860/texas-annexation.

"Bessemer Process." *Encyclopedia Britannica.* Last modified June 20, 2016. https://www.britannica.com/technology/Bessemer-process.

"Biography of Susan B. Anthony." National Susan B. Anthony House and Museum. Accessed February 2, 2018. http://susanbanthonyhouse.org/her-story/biography.php.

Carnegie, Andrew. *The Autobiography of Andrew Carnegie.* Ann Arbor, MI: Northeastern Press University, 1986.

———. *The Gospel of Wealth Essays and Other Writings.* New York: Penguin Classics, 2006.

Carnes, Mark C., and John A. Garraty. *American Destiny Narrative of a Nation Volume I to 1877.* New York: Pearson Longman, 2006.

———. *American Destiny Narrative of a Nation Volume II Since 1865.* New York: Pearson Longman, 2006.

"Consumer Price Index (Estimate) 1800." Federal Reserve Bank of Minneapolis. Accessed February 2, 2018. https://www.minneapolisfed.org/community/financial-and-economic-education/cpi-calculator-information/consumer-price-index-1800.

"Edwin Drake American Oil Driller." *Encyclopedia Britannica.* Last modified September 27, 2016. https://www.britannica.com/biography/Edwin-Laurentine-Drake.

"Ellis Island History." The Statue of Liberty Ellis Island Foundation, Inc. Accessed February 8, 2018. https://www.libertyellisfoundation.org/ellis-island-history#Origin.

"Financial Panic of 1873." US Department of the Treasury. Accessed February 14, 2018. https://www.treasury.gov/about/education/Pages/Financial-Panic-of-1873.aspx.

"Henry Clay Frick." *Encyclopedia Britannica.* Last modified January 31, 2018. https://www.britannica.com/biography/Henry-Clay-Frick.

"Historical Essay Wisconsin (state)." Wisconsin Historical Society. Accessed January 31, 2018. https://www.wisconsinhistory.org/Records/Article/CS1807.

"History of the Pledge." The Giving Pledge. Accessed February 16, 2018. https://givingpledge.org/About.aspx.

"Immigration and Citizenship Data." US Citizenship and Immigration Services. Accessed February 2, 2018. https://www.uscis.gov/tools/reports-studies/immigration-forms-data.

"The Inside History of the Carnegie Steel Company." University of Pittsburgh Press. Accessed February 10, 2018. http://www.upress.pitt.edu/BookDetails.aspx?bookId=34335.

"John D. Rockefeller American Industrialist." *Encyclopedia Britannica*. Last modified January 25, 2018. https://www.britannica.com/biography/John-D-Rockefeller.

"John D. Rockefeller Biography." Biography. Accessed February 14, 2018. https://www.biography.com/people/john-d-rockefeller-20710159.

"J. P. Morgan American Financier." *Encyclopedia Britannica*. Last modified January 26, 2018. https://www.britannica.com/biography/J-P-Morgan.

McGillem, Clare D. "Telegraph." *Encyclopedia Britannica*. Last modified December 7, 2016. https://www.britannica.com/technology/telegraph.

McPherson, James. "A Brief Overview of the American Civil War: A Defining Time in Our Nation's History." Civil War Trust. Accessed February 6, 2018. https://www.civilwar.org/learn/articles/brief-overview-american-civil-war.

"Mexican-American War." *Encyclopedia Britannica*. Last modified July 21, 2017. https://www.britannica.com/event/Mexican-American-War#accordion-article-history.

"Muckrakers." Khan Academy. Accessed February 16, 2018. https://www.khanacademy.org/humanities/ap-us-history/period-7/apush-age-of-empire/a/muckrakers.

"Network to Freedom." Erie Canalway National Heritage Corridor. Accessed February 5, 2018. https://eriecanalway.org/learn/history-culture/social-reform/ugrr.

"Our History." Carnegie Institute for Science. Accessed February 15, 2018. https://carnegiescience.edu/about/history.

"Pennsylvania Railroad Company." *Encyclopedia Britannica.* Last modified April 5, 2016. https://www.britannica.com/topic/Pennsylvania-Railroad-Company.

"Primary Documents in American History: Louisiana Purchase." The Library of Congress. Last modified April 26, 2017. https://www.loc.gov/rr/program/bib/ourdocs/Louisiana.html.

"Scottish Emigration 1830s–1939." BBC. Accessed February 16, 2018. https://www.bbc.co.uk/education/guides/z4h39j6/revision/2.

"Triumphant Democracy: US Railroads." Harvard University. Accessed February 15, 2018. https://www.library.hbs.edu/hc/railroads/us-railroads.html.

"U.S. History and Historical Documents." USA.gov. Last modified July 25, 2017. https://www.usa.gov/history.

"U.S. Immigration Since 1965." History.com. Accessed February 8, 2018. http://www.history.com/topics/us-immigration-since-1965.

"War of 1812–1815." Office of the Historian. https://history.state.gov/milestones/1801-1829/war-of-1812.

"Wealthiest Man in the World." Carnegie Corporation of New York. Accessed February 14, 2018. https://www.carnegie.org/interactives/foundersstory/#!/#wealthiest-man-world.

# INDEX

Page numbers in **boldface** refer to images.

# ABOUT THE AUTHOR

**Kaitlin Scirri** is a writer and editor of books for children, teens, and adults. She holds a bachelor's degree in writing from the State University of New York at Buffalo State. Other books by Scirri include *Civic Values: Property Rights*, *The Science of Superpowers: Invisibility and X-Ray Vision*, and *The Science of Superpowers: Controlling Electricity and Weather*. An avid reader, Scirri has a deep love and appreciation of libraries and was thrilled to write about Andrew Carnegie and his contributions to libraries and education.